What's the Buzz?

Some children, for all manner of reasons, struggle to make friends and fit in socially. *What's the Buzz?* is a unique sixteen-lesson social skills enrichment programme designed to explicitly teach children how to think and relate to others in social situations.

This lively, highly practical role-play and play-based programme targets everyday themes: how to greet, make and keep friends, fit in, read one's own emotions, read the feelings of others, deal with competition and cope with worry, frustration and disappointment more constructively. Based on an extensive body of research believed to stimulate social thinking and accomplish powerful outcomes, *What's the Buzz?* is:

- **S**equenced – it follows a logical breakdown of each skill
- **A**ctive – it uses role-plays and rehearsal with feedback
- **F**ocused – it dedicates time solely towards teaching a specific skill
- **E**xplicit – it teaches a specific social/emotional skill each session.

The programme has proven wide appeal to teachers, counsellors, psychologists, teaching assistants, support staff and parent volunteers in schools. While tailored for small specific groups of children, it also has a broader multi-purpose scope with larger mainstream classes. Each lesson also includes extensive notes offering parents and teachers handy ideas to reinforce the themes presented.

This book is complemented by the website **www.whatsthebuzz.net.au** which offers online training modules and a wealth of other resources.

Mark Le Messurier is an educator, counsellor, author and conference presenter. He works in private practice and in schools supporting teachers and students, and is a recipient of the prestigious Australian National Excellence in Teaching Award. www.marklemessurier.com.au

Madhavi Nawana Parker is a behaviour consultant in private practice for children with Asperger Syndrome, Attention Disorders and Learning Difficulties and regularly presents training workshops throughout Australia for parents, teachers and allied health professionals. www.madhavinawana.com.au

'I trialed the program and found it great to use. I liked its consistency, its commitment to collecting evidence-based data and explicit teaching of the skill followed by practice activities. The variety of social games and activities were fantastic and I now use many of these across other therapy settings.'

Donna, clinical psychologist

'*What's the Buzz?* teaches invaluable life lessons, strategically disguised as fun and play for kids. From social isolation to enjoying school playtimes – we have been just amazed at the transformation in our six-year-old child's social skills.'

Heather, mother

'Our daughter thoroughly enjoyed this innovative program. We think it has been effective as she's jumped forward in leaps and bounds. Her understanding of herself and others, and her social confidence has blossomed.'

Bennett, father

'*What's the Buzz?* has been an amazing gift. Step by step we witnessed our son reach new milestones. He has become so much more confident, happier and socially interested.'

Angie, Founding Chairperson,
The Gold Foundation

'We have used *What's the Buzz?* over the past two years. It has developed confidence, social skills and resilience in participating students. Parents and teachers have also benefited from the weekly tips to encourage continuity between the sessions, school and home.'

Virginia Evans, Head of Pulteney Grammar School,
Kurrajong, Adelaide, South Australia

'Our *What's the Buzz?* pilot programme was a huge success. Parents frequently commented on the positive social changes stimulated within their children. Participants enjoyed it, and many took their new skills to school and used them to relate to friends in friendlier ways. This programme is a gem; valuable, adaptable and easy to implement!'

Kathryn Hurrell, Senior Respite Coordinator,
City of Onkaparinga, Adelaide,
South Australia

What's the Buzz?

A social skills enrichment programme for primary students

*Mark Le Messurier and
Madhavi Nawana Parker*

*Illustrations by
Lauren Eldridge-Murray*

Routledge
Taylor & Francis Group

LONDON AND NEW YORK

Intellectual property

Precisely determining the intellectual ownership of many of the social games included within the programme is difficult. Most have emerged as party games and team building ideas and, over generations, have been modified and adjusted to suit particular needs. Wherever possible the games with traceable sources have been acknowledged. However, if by chance, an original source has been omitted we sincerely apologise. The overriding motivation has been to develop a balanced repertoire of playful games that benefit the socialisation of young people.

Access to online content and training www.whatsthebuzz.net.au

The material within this book may only be photocopied and used by the purchasing individual or organisation. Online registration for *What's the Buzz?* training is recommended and may be accessed through www.whatsthebuzz.net.au For a small cost, registered facilitators gain a deeper appreciation of the programme and how best to deliver it. Registration also offers online TRAINING MODULES, access to the images, games, role-play cards, certificates, worksheets, survey forms and an option to measure each participant's progress using a specialised online facility. These can be amended and personalised to suit particular situations or individual needs. The files downloaded are protected by copyright and must remain wholly with the registered facilitator. They may not be copied or reproduced in any way, or transmitted to other persons or parties. Registration also offers online accreditation and opportunities to contact the authors of the programme for coaching and advice. In addition, the authors offer a *What's the Buzz?* training day to provide participants with full workshop accreditation.

First edition published 2011
by Routledge
2 Park Square, Milton Park, Abingdon, Oxon, OX14 4RN

Simultaneously published in the USA and Canada
by Routledge
711 Third Avenue, New York, NY 10017

Routledge is an imprint of the Taylor & Francis Group, an informa business

© 2011 Mark Le Messurier and Madhavi Nawana Parker

The right of Mark Le Messurier and Madhavi Nawana Parker to be identified as authors of this work has been asserted by them in accordance with sections 77 and 78 of the Copyright, Designs and Patents Act 1988.

British Library Cataloguing in Publication Data
A catalogue record for this book is available from the British Library

Library of Congress Cataloging-in-Publication Data
Le Messurier, Mark.
  What's the buzz?: games and activities to improve social skills: a 16-lesson plan
  for primary schools/Mark Le Messurier and Madhavi Nawana Parker. – 1st ed.
    p. cm.
  Includes bibliographical references.
  1. Social skills – Study and teaching (Preschool). 2. Social skills – Study
  and teaching (Primary). I. Parker, Madhavi Nawana. II. Title.
  LB1139.S6L4 2011
  372.83 – dc22   2010038184

ISBN13: 978–0–415–58382–4 (pbk)
ISBN13: 978–0–203–82911–0 (ebk)

Typeset in Bembo and Franklin Gothic by
Florence Production Ltd, Stoodleigh, Devon

Printed and bound in Great Britain by the MPG Books Group

Contents

Photocopiable and online resources

A quick guide to the games

Lesson 1: Meeting People and Exiting
- Back to Back (exciting for all ages)
- Name Train (exciting for younger students)
- Greetings and Goodbyes (passive for younger students)
- Greetings! (passive for older students)

Lesson 2: Getting Attention
- Fighting for Attention (exciting for all ages)
- Wild Animals (exciting for all ages)
- Two Truths, One Lie (passive for older students)
- Sleeping Pirate (passive for younger students)

Lesson 3: Following Instructions
- Scavenger Hunt (passive for all ages)
- Port and Starboard (exciting for all ages)
- Mr and Mrs Wright (exciting for all ages)

Lesson 4: Being Friendly
- 'Yes' and 'No' (passive for all ages)
- Mixed-up Body Parts (passive for all ages)
- Catching the Dragon's Tail (exciting for all ages)

Lesson 5: Competition, Winning and Losing
- Tower of Cards (passive for older students)
- Newspaper Race (exciting for all ages)
- Musical Chairs (exciting for all ages)
- Animal Relay (exciting for younger students)
- Ball of String Relay (exciting for older students)
- Can You Guess? (exciting for all ages)

Lesson 6: Identifying Feelings
- What's on a Face? (passive for all ages)
- Guess My Feeling? (passive for older students)
- Cowboys and Indians (exciting for all ages)

Lesson 7: Feelings and the Warning Signs
- Moods (passive for older students)
- Who Am I? (passive for all ages)
- The Detective and the Thief (passive for all ages)

Lesson 8: Feelings and Thinking Positively
- Find the Leader (passive for all ages)
- Minefield (exciting for all ages)
- Chinese Whispers (passive for all ages)

Lesson 9: Feelings and Ideas to Create Well-Being
- Poker Face (exciting for all ages)
- Card Games: Old Maid/Uno/Donkey/Animal Snap (passive for all ages)
- 'Good Morning Mr. President' (passive for all ages)
- Kim's Game (passive for all ages)

Lesson 10: Empathy, Responding to Others
- Who Is It? (passive for all ages)
- Boxes (passive for older students)
- Silly Sally/Silly Sam (passive for all ages)

Lesson 11: Handling Worry
- Walking and Talking (passive for all ages)
- Wink Murder (exciting for older students)
- Bobsledding (exciting for all ages)

Lesson 12: Dealing with Disappointment
- Guard the Pin (exciting for all ages)
- Statues (exciting for all ages)
- 20 Questions, or Fewer (passive for all ages)

Lesson 13: Responding to Bullying
- Lonely Little Ghost (exciting for all ages)
- Draw Me if You Can? (passive for older students)
- Blowing Bubbles (exciting for all ages)

Lesson 14: The Connecting Art of Conversation
- Talk, Listen, Cooperate and Create (passive for all ages)
- Talking about Henny's Coloured Eggs (exciting for all ages)
- Stand in the Line (passive for all ages)

Lesson 15: Learning to 'Fit in'
- Red Letter (exciting for all ages)
- Guess What I'm Drawing? (passive for all ages)
- Dare to Dream? (passive for older students)

Lesson 16: Giving and Receiving Compliments
- Ooh–Ahh (exciting for all ages)
- What I Like About You (passive for all ages)
- All In (exciting for all ages)

About the authors

Mark

Mark Le Messurier is a teacher, counsellor, author and conference presenter. His background spans twenty years in schools and includes special education, adult education, child-centred education and community education projects. Mark is the recipient of a prestigious Australian National Excellence in Teaching Award.

Mark works in schools and in private practice at Fullarton House with children and adolescents he affectionately refers to as the Tough Kids; the kids whose lives are much tougher than most and in the process make life tougher for those who care for them and educate them. They comprise a challenging population of students who are increasingly being identified with underlying executive functioning delays. Without adequate executive functioning capabilities kids lack the ability to delay gratification, listen and filter out distractions, process new information, remember, plan, persist, adapt to change, keep track of time and self-regulate emotion and behaviour. In his book *Teaching Tough Kids* (2010) Mark provides practical, tactical and therapeutic interventions to strengthen the performance of such students; *Teaching Tough Kids* encapsulates the work he is passionate about.

Mark regularly presents at conferences for public and independent schools, parents and interested groups throughout Australasia. His presentations relate to mentoring, AD(H)D, Asperger Syndrome, Specific Learning Difficulties, developing emotional resilience, parenting and teaching children with challenging behaviours.

In 2004 he wrote *Cognitive Behavioural Training: A how-to guide for successful behaviour*. This popular resource addresses common problems that students face: organisation, remembering, self-awareness, motivation and emotional resilience. Mark has also completed a training and development film on Learning Difficulties – *Reflections on Dyslexia*. The package, which also contains a staff development handbook, is available to individuals, schools, colleges and tertiary institutions.

In 2007 *Parenting Tough Kids* was released. It is a book for parents, parent resource libraries, teachers and school counsellors; in fact for anyone with an investment in children. It has also become a popular book in Australia. In 2008 Mark and Lindy Petersen's *STOP and THINK Friendship DVD Package*, first released in 2000, was revised and reprinted. This social skills development resource is also distributed to schools, educators and clinicians throughout Australia, New Zealand and Europe.

Mark is also the architect of the unique *Mentoring Program* currently building capacity in South Australian Catholic schools. The programme provides opportunities for interested staff members to develop skills so they are equipped to mentor students who are experiencing learning, social or behavioural difficulties. These students, aged from 6 to 18 years of age, often 'do it tough' and benefit from the on-going friendship and encouragement from a caring adult working within the school system. Since its inception five years ago, a number of highly skilled school personnel are taking extra care of some of the most vulnerable students in schools, helping to ensure their attachment to the school culture.

Now that *What's the Buzz? A social skills enrichment programme for primary students* is complete, Mark and Madhavi's next project is to develop *What's the Buzz? A social thinking enrichment programme for adolescents.* Both programmes are based on the social thinking workshops they have run for some time.

Mark can be contacted at: www.marklemessurier.com.au and mark@marklemessurier.com.au

Madhavi

Madhavi Nawana Parker began her work in social skills training in 1996 after completing her degree in Psychology and Post Graduate Diploma in Rehabilitation Counselling.

Between the years of 1996 and 2001 she worked as the Social Skills Program Coordinator for Autism SA. Autism SA is a state-wide service providing specialised support for families and schools living and working with individuals with Autism and Asperger Syndrome. Her role involved developing and facilitating social skills programmes throughout Adelaide as well as advising schools and other organisations of appropriate ways to encourage the social and emotional development in this client group.

Madhavi commenced private practice in 2001 at the Behavioural Medicine Institute of Australia. While continuing work in the area of Asperger Syndrome, Madhavi extended her practice to offering service to children and adolescents with Attention Deficit Disorder and Anxiety specialising in social skills training and positive behaviour management principles. Following the birth of her daughter Madhavi continued her private work at Fullarton House where she practices today.

Madhavi is frequently contracted as a behaviour consultant for Catholic Education and the Association of Independent Schools of South Australia. Her role involves working with principals, special education coordinators, counsellors, chaplains, teachers and school psychologists to address the unique needs of socially and emotionally challenged students. Madhavi consults with a mission to develop positive structures within the lives of young people. She also facilitates social skills training groups using the *What's the Buzz?* programme in schools across Australia.

Madhavi presents regularly at conferences to teachers, special education workers, community workers, parents and allied health professionals. Topics include social skills training, positive behaviour management techniques, anxiety and anger management. Madhavi lives in Adelaide, South Australia, with her husband James, daughter Soraya and son Toby.

Madhavi can be contacted at: www.madhavinawana.com.au and madhavi@chariot.net.au

Acknowledgements

Thank you to our actors who volunteered their time and talent to teach others about facial expressions: Alannah, Amelia, Antonio, Bailey, Catherine, Dylan, Elana, Grace, Max, Nethli, Sofia, Soraya and Thomas.

We would like to acknowledge David Worswick Photography, Adelaide.

Thank you to family, friends and colleages for guidance and loyal support.

Introduction

Why teach social skills?

For most, the foundation for social thinking is hard-wired at birth setting the stage for rich development over a lifetime of social interactions with others. Nearly all of us learn how to interpret the messages behind the actions and words of others, and how to respond using appropriate social skills. We grasp the consequence of thinking socially and understand it is the forerunner to every social encounter – how we speak, share, take turns, gesture, discuss, use space, stand, walk, develop friendships, cope with disappointment and boredom, even how we relate to a pet, movie or novel. As our social thinking develops we begin to integrate the thoughts, feelings and intent of others as a vital part of our world.

For a variety of reasons some children find it much harder to think socially and use their social tools suitably when it really counts. Yet, those of us who work with children struggling to understand the social world see that beneath their displays of frustration and clumsiness is usually a yearning to fit in, find friendships and be accepted. By the time children reach adolescence the longing to fit in and interact truly intensifies (Church *et al.*, 2003). The results of clinical studies point out what we have long suspected, and that is, without reasonable social success children and adolescents are more likely to be at risk from emotional and mental health difficulties (Hay *et al.*, 2004). The ability to create and foster friendship, accompanied by opportunities to feel accepted by others, is significant.

A body of well regarded studies reveal that teaching social thinking to young people with social delay is invaluable towards improving their capacity to interact with others (Garcia Winner, 2003). A study by Jenkins and Batgidou emphasised the importance of directly teaching social skills to young individuals with Attention Disorders (Jenkins and Batgidou, 2003). They found that without specific social training these children actually remained developmentally delayed in social knowledge. Similar research evaluating the use of social skills training for children with Asperger Syndrome established that following a twelve-week programme incorporating role-play, social discussions and activities promoting social interaction there was a significant improvement in the participants' social competence (Tse *et al.*, 2007). The same clinical study

1

also found an unexpected improvement in difficult behaviours such as irritability and hyperactivity following the programme. A review of 317 Social and Emotional Learning (SEL) programmes involving 324,303 students for the 'Collaborative for Academic, Social and Emotional Learning' (CASEL) definitively summarised the value of such programmes (Payten *et al.*, 2008). The programmes reviewed, which included whole class training approaches and smaller group settings, showed measurable gains for students with and without social, emotional and behavioural difficulties. An encouraging outcome was a reduction in behavioural problems and emotional distress for participants. SEL programmes also positively influenced the overall academic engagement and performance of students (Diekstra, 2008; www.casel.org). Most recently, John Hattie, in his ground-breaking book *Visible Learning*, provided educators with state-of-the-art evidence about the greatest influences on student learning and engagement. With respect to social skills programmes he states, 'Social skills programs can make a positive difference to social outcomes' (Hattie, 2009, p. 150). His evidence, based on 84 studies and 27,064 students, indicates that the most effective programmes employ coaching, direct modelling and obvious feedback, and focus particularly on individual peer relation issues.

What is this programme?

What's the Buzz? is a social skills enrichment programme designed to explicitly teach children to think socially and improve their ability to interact socially. It is a 16-lesson role-play and play-based programme for children aged between 8 and 12 years. The programme is designed to assist children to gain insight into:

- how essential social conventions work (the social thinking of others)

- why people think and react in the way they do (how their social mind works)

- understanding their own feelings and the feelings of others (feelings drive behaviour)

- what their behaviour causes others to think of them (the consequences of behaviour)

- the reasons why others respond to them in the way they do (what others are looking for socially)

- how to adjust their behaviour so life is more enjoyable (social referencing).

The direct method of instruction embedded within our programme is based on an extensive body of current research referred to by the acronym 'SAFE' (Durlak *et al.*, 2008). Such programmes are deliberately structured to achieve maximum effect. They are:

- **S**equenced – follow a logical step-by-step breakdown of each skill

- **A**ctive – use role-plays or behavioural rehearsal with feedback

- **F**ocused – dedicate a period of time solely towards teaching a specific skill

- **E**xplicit – teach a specific social/emotional skill each session.

What's the Buzz? breaks each skill into individual components and directly models them so students can see how they look and sound. Social thinking is also highlighted through role-play, rehearsal, feedback and play-based activities in the context of either a small group or as a whole class approach. In this way children gain the under-standings, the language and confidence required to transfer the newly acquired skills to other settings (Attwood, 2007; Durlak *et al.*, 2008; Godfrey *et al.*, 2005). The efficacy of whether an encouraging small group situation or a whole class approach provides students with optimal opportunity to transfer new skills into real life settings remains somewhat contentious. Our experience and interpretation of the literature suggests there is scope for both approaches. What will determine the effective conversion of new skills into real life interactions is the quality of direct instruction students receive, the confidence they develop along the way, the personal desire they have to incorporate new skills and make changes, the optimism that peers in the group or class are responding with around them, and the ongoing support of significant others in their lives such as teachers and parents. Clearly, the notion of providing a social skills programme without adequate continuing support and encouragement in the classroom and at home possesses obvious limitations. This is why each lesson from *What's the Buzz?* includes extensive notes *(After the Buzz: social thinking ideas for parents)* offering parents an assortment of practical ideas to work with at home. This is also why we recommend sending a copy of the lesson itself home to parents each week.

What is the content?

What's the Buzz? encourages children to think and act pro-socially.

First term	**Second term**
(approximately forty-five minutes per lesson)	(approximately forty-five minutes per lesson)
Lesson 1: Meeting People and Exiting	Lesson 9: Feelings and Ideas to Create Well-Being
Lesson 2: Getting Attention	Lesson 10: Empathy, Responding to Others
Lesson 3: Following Instructions	Lesson 11: Handling Worry
Lesson 4: Being Friendly	Lesson 12: Dealing with Disappointment
Lesson 5: Competition, Winning and Losing	Lesson 13: Responding to Bullying
Lesson 6: Identifying Feelings	Lesson 14: The Connecting Art of Conversation
Lesson 7: Feelings and the Warning Signs	Lesson 15: Learning to 'Fit in'
Lesson 8: Feelings and Thinking Positively	Lesson 16: Giving and Receiving Compliments

The programme is designed for lessons to be presented sequentially, either with whole class groups or with smaller targeted groups. While a sequential presentation is our recommendation, some scope exists for educators to select individual lessons or activities to strengthen a particular set of communication skills identified within mainstream class groups.

Will the programme fix 'bad behaviour'?

This programme is not a cure-all for taming 'bad behaviour'. *What's the Buzz?* is a social skills enrichment programme designed as a structured framework for group interaction. Its focus is one that allows young people to learn more about themselves, more about others and develop communication skills. It will almost certainly fail if seized upon to remedy the unruly behaviours of a group of so-called 'naughty boys'. Its success hinges on the careful selection of children who may have degrees of social, emotional and behavioural challenges, but above all are likely to form a bond, likely to learn, likely to enjoy one another's company and will receive continuing support from adults in the classroom and at home.

Who is suitable to participate?

Children who are selected for the programme are those who struggle to make friends and fit in socially. Often they lack confidence, find it difficult to go with the flow, react too quickly, struggle to read the social play, to bounce back after upsets and deal with day to day frustrations appropriately. In essence, they have trouble making sense of how the social systems they interact with work; the family system, the school system or the friends system.

What's the Buzz? has proven to be particularly helpful for children with higher-functioning forms of autism spectrum disorders, such as Asperger syndrome. Similarly, those diagnosed with language disorder, specific learning difficulties, non-verbal learning disorder, pervasive developmental disorder – not otherwise specified, ADHD, reactive behaviours, anxiety, shyness and social phobia have also benefited.

What else is of value about the programme?

The 50 social skill building games within the programme have become popular choices for teachers of mainstream classes to build class unity and social cohesion. Used as energisers, icebreakers and team building activities these certainly have the capacity to positively switch the emotional climate of the classroom.

Who can facilitate the programme?

What's the Buzz? is intended for use in schools by teachers, school counsellors, school psychologists, teacher assistants, support staff, parent volunteers and allied health professionals. It also has wide application in a range of private clinical settings; psychologists, counsellors, speech pathologists, occupational therapists, social workers, play therapists and so on. Those who wish to take on the role of a facilitator and have been trained in Circle Time, use Circle Time practices or have an understanding of Circle Time values are ideally positioned to run *What's the Buzz?* (Roffey, 2006). They understand the role of a facilitator, someone who encourages the group to develop their own solutions rather than being a controller.

Is training recommended?

You will find everything you need in this book to run a successful programme. Training is highly desirable as it helps to ensure the highest quality of delivery to children and families. For training, access www.whatsthebuzz.net.au Alternatively, contact Mark Le Messurier (mark@marklemessurier.com.au) or Madhavi Nawana Parker (madhavi@chariot.net.au) directly.

A comprehensive online training option that offers online accreditation, as well as a full day workshop delivered by the authors is available at www.whatsthebuzz. net.au

Is the programme easy to follow?

The programme is straightforward to use. The nature of schools is that staff are always pressed for time, so for a programme to work it must be easy to absorb, easy to organise materials and easy to place into action. By following the programme's structure facilitators quickly build familiarity. This enhances the capacity to deliver information accurately to students. Equally, the receptiveness of students is heightened due to their sense of predictability about the programme. With this in mind, each lesson is presented within the following design:

- topic
- explanation; alerts facilitator(s) to the key skill components to be delivered to students
- materials required for the lesson
- THE LESSON:
    1   *What's the Buzz?* – introduces students to the topic and the new set of skills to be learned.
    2   *Show me the Buzz* – gives students the opportunity to practise and show they understand the new skill set.
    3   *Do you know the Buzz?* – a fast-moving quiz or question time for students to consolidate key concepts.
    4   *The Buzz* – students play social games to have fun together, and build their newly learned skills.

5   *Goodbye Buzz* – an organisational aid to finish the lesson on.

6   *After the Buzz: social thinking ideas for parents* – offers sensible advice and useful ideas that can be placed into practice at home to build onto the skills introduced in the lesson.

7   Photocopiable and online resources are located at the end of most lessons ready to be photocopied; alternatively, they can be downloaded from www.whatsthebuzz.net.au.

A closing word

Beyond seeing children trial new ways to think socially and reach for emotionally healthier futures, there are two other benefits that consistently arise from *What's the Buzz?* First are the warm interactions between students and the formation of new relationships. This is heartening, because many of the participants find it difficult to build friendships in the highly dynamic school environment. Second, is the obvious continuing support and encouragement parents gain from *After the Buzz: social thinking ideas for parents.* Parents repeatedly remark how helpful the ideas and approaches embedded in this segment of the programme are to them at home.

Photocopiable resources now follow, and don't forget the online resources at www.whatsthebuzz.net.au!

What's the Buzz?

Introductory letter and consent for parents and caregivers

Date ....

Dear ....

We look forward to the opportunity to participate with you and your child in *What's the Buzz?* It is a unique social thinking programme that encourages children to think about how to get along with others and explore the benefits of developing new social skills.

What is involved?

The aim is for your son or daughter to have sixteen 45-minute sessions over two school terms to build on to their social and emotional thinking. This will take place within a SMALL GROUP or as a CLASS GROUP (circle the option decided). The programme will be delivered through direct teaching, role-play, quizzes and fun in the context of an encouraging group. *What's the Buzz?* aims to teach primary aged children 'how-to':

- meet people, be friendly and hold a conversation

- give compliments and show care

- seek attention in constructive ways

- understand their own feelings

- 'read' the feelings of others

- take turns, be calmer under pressure, handle loss and disappointment with poise

- deal with worry

- thoughtfully respond to rejection and bullying

- always apply positive thinking to fix problems

- cope more resiliently with the inevitable emotional highs and lows that life offers.

What's the Buzz?

Introductory letter and consent for parents and caregivers *continued . . .*

Programmed topics

Lesson 1: Meeting People and Exiting

Lesson 2: Getting Attention

Lesson 3: Following Instructions

Lesson 4: Being Friendly

Lesson 5: Competition, Winning and Losing

Lesson 6: Identifying Feelings

Lesson 7: Feelings and the Warning Signs

Lesson 8: Feelings and Thinking Positively

Lesson 9: Feelings and Ideas to Create Well-Being

Lesson 10: Empathy, Responding to Others

Lesson 11: Handling Worry

Lesson 12: Dealing with Disappointment

Lesson 13: Responding to Bullying

Lesson 14: The Connecting Art of Conversation

Lesson 15: Learning to 'Fit in'

Lesson 16: Giving and Receiving Compliments

What is your role?

Your role is invaluable and we welcome your communication. So that you know what your child experiences in each lesson, notes will be sent home every week. The notes should include a copy of the lesson itself and a section called, *After the Buzz: social thinking ideas for parents*. It offers useful advice that can be gently placed into practice at home to add value to what your child is learning.

Usually a 'parents only' meeting is scheduled in week 2 or 3 of *What's the Buzz?* to discuss the nature of the programme and gather information. A second meeting to conclude is likely to be held around week 15. Your facilitator(s) will advise you about these meetings a little later. In the meantime, would you kindly fill out and sign the consent. Also, please complete the parent PRE-GROUP social functioning survey, and arrange for your child and your child's teacher to complete theirs. A prompt return is appreciated.

If you have questions, concerns or vital information that should be known prior to the first session, do not hesitate to contact a facilitator.

What's the Buzz?

Introductory letter and consent for parents and caregivers *continued . . .*

Your child's *What's the Buzz?* facilitator(s) is/are

....

Their contact is

....

....

Your child's first session is scheduled to start on (date and time)

....

at (place)

....

Sign and return the section below to school or to a *What's the Buzz?* facilitator.

✂ — Cut here.

What's the Buzz? Parental/caregiver consent
For your child to participate in the programme a parent or guardian must sign this consent section and return it.

We seek your permission for (child's name)

....

to be involved in *What's the Buzz?*

By signing this we assume you have read the information attached to this consent and give permission for information to be shared, respectfully and confidentially, between teachers and facilitators during this time.

Parent/Caregiver's name

....

Parent/Caregiver's signature

....

Date ....

What's the Buzz?

Teacher form

PRE-GROUP social functioning survey

Child's name _____   Date _____

Teacher's name _____   Phone _____

School _____   Age/year level _____

Circle the number displayed with each question or statement that 'feels about right' based on your observations. Also, please circle any key words in the questions and statements that highlight a particular concern.

1 = no/never   2 = hardly ever/a bit   3 = mostly/a lot   4 = certainly/yes

1. Is the student accepted by peers?
        1   2   3   4

2. Do you think this student has the desire to make friends?
        1   2   3   4

3. Does the student notice the behaviours of others and try to 'fit in' with them?
        1   2   3   4

4. The student looks for relationships, but is unsuccessful
        1   2   3   4

5. Do you think this student is happy enough, socially?
        1   2   3   4

6. This student understands how to 'read' and respond to the emotions of others
        1   2   3   4

7. Does the student deal with conflict and disagreements between peers appropriately?
        1   2   3   4

8. The student follows instructions and completes tasks appropriately
        1   2   3   4

9. Does the student have learning difficulties, a short attention span or is distractible?
        1   2   3   4

10. This student displays (circle appropriate words) anger, crying, sulking, shyness, hitting, running away, biting, withdrawing, verbal abuse when things go wrong?
        1   2   3   4

11. Ideally, I hope this student can learn to _____

_____

_____

The information you have shared may be viewed by the student's parents.
Please return before the first lesson. **Thank you!**

What's the Buzz?

Parent form

PRE-GROUP social functioning survey

Child's name _____   Date _____

Parent's name _____   Phone _____

School _____   Age/year level _____

Circle the number displayed with each question or statement that 'feels about right' based on your observations. Also, please circle any key words in the questions and statements that highlight a particular concern.

1 = no/never   2 = hardly ever/a bit   3 = mostly/a lot   4 = certainly/yes

1. Does your child have friends at school?
       1   2   3   4

2. Do you think they have the ability/desire to make friends and be a friend?
       1   2   3   4

3. My child is able to establish relationships, maintain them and enjoy them
       1   2   3   4

4. My child is able to 'fit in' with others and 'go with the flow'
       1   2   3   4

5. My child is happy with their own company. They do not seek relationships with others
       1   2   3   4

6. My child reads the emotions and feelings of others suitably
       1   2   3   4

7. My child handles disagreements and conflicts constructively
       1   2   3   4

8. My child has a short attention span, is often distracted and is very active
       1   2   3   4

9. I think *What's the Buzz?* is a forum likely to be enjoyed by my child
       1   2   3   4

10. My child is prone to (circle appropriate words) anger, crying, sulking, shyness, hitting, running away, biting, withdrawing, verbal abuse when things go wrong?
       1   2   3   4

11. Has your child completed assessments that may be helpful?   (yes / no)
    Can you share these with us?   (yes / no)

The information you have shared may be viewed by your child's teacher.
Please return before the first lesson. **Thank you!**

What's the Buzz?
Student form

PRE-GROUP *social functioning survey*

Your name _____ Age/year level _____

Teacher's name/class _____ School _____

Circle the number below each question that 'feels right' to you

There are no right or wrong answers because this is about how you feel, and how you see things

1 = no/never   2 = hardly ever/a bit   3 = mostly/a lot   4 = certainly/yes

1. Do you have friends to play with at school?
   1   2   3   4

2. Are you liked by children?
   1   2   3   4

3. Once you make a friend, do you happily keep the friendship?
   1   2   3   4

4. Do you get too excited, too silly or too bossy around other children?
   1   2   3   4

5. Do you feel too shy or worried to make friends?
   1   2   3   4

6. Do you get confused trying to work out the feelings of other kids?
   1   2   3   4

7. Do you get so annoyed when someone is mean to you that you handle it badly?
   1   2   3   4

8. Is it easy to talk to children your own age and get along with them?
   1   2   3   4

9. Is it hard to concentrate and get your work done at school?
   1   2   3   4

10. When things go wrong do you get very upset? Do you cry, sulk, get angry or hurt others?
    1   2   3   4

11. I hope *What's the Buzz?* can help me to _____

_____

_____

If you want help to do this survey ask Mum, Dad, your teacher or your *What's the Buzz?* facilitator. This information may be seen by your parents or teacher. Please return as soon as you can. Thank you!

Practical considerations for implementation as a small group initiative or a whole class strategy

Getting started

To begin, we suggest sending a copy of the

- Introductory letter and consent

- TEACHER FORM: pre-group social functioning survey (even if you are the class teacher running *What's the Buzz?* with your class we recommend that you fill out a form for each child in order to gather some baseline data)

- PARENT FORM: pre-group social functioning survey

- STUDENT FORM: pre-group social functioning survey (older students are capable of filling out the survey and usually enjoy it. Younger children require helpful prompting from a teacher or parent)

to parents and teachers at least a week before the programme commences. This allows time for discussion and questions. Consent and survey forms can be returned by fax, mail, scanned and emailed or hand delivered. The feedback from TEACHERS, PARENTS and STUDENTS collected in these initial surveys establishes a benchmark of opinion about each child's social functioning. Be mindful to work within the protocols expected by your system.

The Introductory letter and consent, the TEACHER FORM: pre-group social functioning survey, the PARENT FORM: pre-group social functioning survey and the STUDENT FORM: pre-group social functioning survey are located in the photocopiable resources at the end of the introduction ready to be photocopied. Alternatively, they can be downloaded from www.whatsthebuzz.net.au and adjusted to meet your requirements.

POST-GROUP social functioning surveys

These surveys, for teachers, parents and students, are located in the photocopiable resources section at the end of Lesson 15. They can also be downloaded from www.whatsthebuzz.net.au and personalised.

There is no reason why the post-group surveys cannot be sent home earlier, perhaps in weeks 13 or 14 of the programme. The data collected from the post-group surveys can be compared to the data collected earlier on in the pre-group surveys. We usually attach a photocopy of the pre-group social functioning survey so teachers, parents and students are able to reflect more accurately. To assist in collating the pre-group and post-group information received for each student the www.whatsthebuzz.net.au website offers a specialised facility to visually compare the data in each area of the child's social functioning. This visual comparison helps us to understand the depth of improvement, and where future challenges remain. It is also a valuable document for facilitators to speak from, and for parents to refer to at the final 'Parents Only meeting'.

As to the question, 'Why collect data, and does it matter?' Yes it does! Increasingly in education today the drive is to measure progress so that the learning experience is transparently quantifiable. It takes the guesswork out of the teaching and learning model. This must be what we strive for; it tells us to what degree we have been successful, where new challenges lie and prompts optimistic talk to plan for a child's future.

Ideal facilitator qualities

We want facilitators to bring their own individuality, flair and experience to the group. While lessons are designed with a regular sequence and explicit content, wonderful scope exists for facilitators to use their unique knowledge and individuality to impart the content. What's more, the group itself, their experiences, ages, interests, personalities and interest in one another will shape the very character and mood of the group.

A facilitator's personal flexibility and aptitude to 'read' a group is paramount. For example, three or four games are offered in *The Buzz* towards the end of each lesson, but often there is only time to play one or two. Additional games have been included so facilitators have a choice as to which activities they feel best meet the group's age, energy and style. Similarly, some days it will be harder to engage the group because they are restless or tired. On these days it is wise to focus on the role-playing activities, quizzes and social games, and curtail the delivery of information and instruction.

The best quality a facilitator can bring to a group is an engaging attitude that says to students, 'I like being here with you.'

Arranging a small target group

Flexible thinking needs to be exercised from the start. To illustrate this, arranging a small targeted group is not as clear-cut as placing five ten-year-old children with a facilitator, simply because they are ten years old. What usually takes priority is an attempt to match the social/emotional/intellectual maturity of each participant, to strike a gender balance (if desirable) and mix personalities with a probability of getting along with one another.

Group size

When small target groups are constructed, we recommend one facilitator for four or five children, and two facilitators for seven or eight children. During the planning phase, the level of challenge expected from the group must be considered. If the group shapes up to look quite challenging keep it smaller. It is far better to run two smaller groups than an oversized, unmanageable group.

Physically arranging the group

Constructing the best possible environment to run this programme successfully is a critical issue. After all, many of the children participating display immature social thinking and distractible behaviours despite being very well meaning. This is of course why they attend! So, positively manipulating the environment to get the best from participants is absolutely strategic, and to downplay it may be perilous.

The best arrangement is to have students and the facilitator(s) sit in a social circle. In this way everyone can see, hear and participate. We usually sit on seats arranged in a circle because there is some anecdotal evidence suggesting improved concentration and enhanced group steadiness when students sit on seats. Nevertheless, the circle formation encourages the group to develop a sense of unity and connectedness. Whatever organising arrangements you feel are necessary, bear in mind that children always feel more settled walking into an environment that is prepared and arranged in the same way every time. This engenders a steadiness that inspires a positive difference for the cohort of children we work with.

Participation

As you would expect, some children take several sessions before feeling secure enough to freely participate. Always allow participants to 'pass' on an activity if reluctant. Remember, some learn best through quiet observation. Occasionally a child will insist on sitting outside the social circle, but will stay in close proximity to the group. We usually accept this in the early stages, but make it clear we would prefer them to be part of the circle. Try not to let this become a matter of consequence. Instead, work on a progressive plan to support the student's entry into the circle over time.

Group rules

The rules are phrased concisely and positively. Just as classroom rules do, they alert group members to what is expected (located in the photocopiable resources at the end of this chapter; alternatively, they can be downloaded from www.whatsthebuzz.net.au). They include:

- Friendly words

- Gentle actions

- Quiet listening

- Try your best.

By introducing group rules at the outset, and restating them briefly at the beginning of each lesson, a clear message about the type of behaviours that are valued is established. This also helps to add an atmosphere of certainty over what is expected.

Group feedback ideas

Being skilful at capturing the cooperative and pro-social behaviours of children is a 'core component' in the delivery of *What's the Buzz?* After all, most of the children participating in the programme display poorly developed social thinking that often results in awkward behaviours. This is of course why they attend. They still have their social thinking and emotional/behavioural learner's plates on! They are dependent on a facilitator who cleverly prompts, reinforces desirable actions and acknowledges when they are doing well. An interactive design most likely to improve outcomes is when the focus is on guiding children towards desired goals in the context of them feeling connected to the people they are learning alongside.

The experts have long told us that nothing influences the behaviour of children in the direction we want to go as well as good quality feedback; catching and commenting on the valued behaviours (Cornelius-White, 2007). One particularly powerful way to do this is to develop a 'token reinforcement system'. This is where a teacher in a classroom, or group facilitator within *What's the Buzz?*, earmarks a set of specific behaviours required from the group – *in our situation the set of specific behaviours are plainly linked to the group rules*. Then, as students display the desired behaviours they each receive a tangible recognition in the form of a symbol or token. Rewards may be involved, although reward alone is not what feedback is about. In fact, students in our groups learn very quickly that regardless of how well they do individually, or as a group, there is no guarantee they will receive a reward at the end of the session. We usually let them know that a small reward is on offer for four out of eight sessions, and the weeks have been predetermined. The research is patently clear; individuals who develop the skills associated with 'social and token reinforcement systems' offer children considerable opportunities to improve intention, perseverance, motivation, awareness and achievement (Hattie, 2009).

There are two fundamental skills associated with catching valued behaviours:

1   delivery of genuine positive verbal feedback (social reinforcement)

2   expertly combine the first with the delivery of a tangible reward system (token reinforcement).

Children and adults alike behave according to the pleasure principle; behaviour that is rewarding tends to continue and behaviour that is unrewarding tends to stop. Think about it, even within the adult world 'token reinforcement systems' are widely used as healthy emotional/behavioural motivators: fair pay for a fair day's work, loyalty cards and vouchers, frequent flyer points and banks running reward schemes for clients who pay their mortgage repayments regularly on time.

Here are several 'token reinforcement systems' we use to catch and maintain a cooperative group spirit. Try one of these or use a novel idea you know works!

What's the Buzz? Group rules cards and feedback cards

First, print the 'Thumbs up feedback' cards (print on several bright orange sheets) and the 'Group rules feedback' cards (print on several red sheets) onto light card, laminate and cut them out (located in the photocopiable resources at the end of this chapter; alternatively they can be downloaded from www.whatsthebuzz.net.au).

At the beginning of the lesson place the cards in front of you in category piles. Organise to have a small business card holder or an unbreakable plastic container in front of each group member or under their chair. When a participant needs reminding to follow a particular 'group rule' they are simply handed one of the 'Group rules – feedback' cards to let them know which behaviour the group is seeking. No words are required. The student places the card into their business card holder or container.

As soon as the student begins to show behaviours that are valued hand them a 'Thumbs up feedback' card. Throughout the lesson continuously hand students 'Thumbs up feedback' cards as feedback for participating in a helpful spirit.

At the end of the session, pool all of the cards students have collected and if there are more 'thumbs up' cards than 'Group rules – feedback' cards, everyone in the group may receive a small reward. It is of course ideal to time the build-up of 'thumbs up' cards to coincide with the end of the lesson.

This approach can be adapted. If one or two of the participants in the group consistently show challenging behaviours adjust the approach so that rewards may be earned on an individual basis.

Lucky gold nuggets

The enticement of gold will positively motivate any group's cooperative spirit!

Make your own set of gold nuggets by painting a selection of common nuggetty rocks with gold spray paint. Next, get hold of a rustic looking container to hold the gold nuggets.

Begin the lesson with the gold nuggets sitting alongside the empty container in the middle of the circle. Whenever you catch something happening within the group that is worthy, comment on it, and ask that student to add a nugget to the container. When the container is filled (try to time this with the end of the lesson) each participant may take home a small reward for showing their cooperative best.

This approach can be adapted as well. Our adaption has been to use smaller gold nuggets and add one or two to a small container placed in front of each child as we catch constructive behaviours. In this way each participant can earn their reward on an individual basis.

Build a friendship wall

Buy twenty plastic cubes about 8 to 12 centimetres in size. They can be cubes that are smooth or lock into one another. If you cannot find plastic have them cut from wood. These become the bricks to build a friendship wall. Write on each brick a highly valued friendship quality: compassion, happiness, respect, helpfulness, honesty, humour, tolerance, easygoingness, optimistic, shares, kindness, loyalty, dependable, fairness, thoughtful, openness, care, fun, sympathy, good listener.

Begin each lesson with the blocks scattered on the floor inside the social circle or on a nearby table. When you catch something happening within the group that is commendable, comment on it, and ask that student to add a brick to the friendship wall. Every so often ask the group why a particular quality is important. Keep on catching the behaviours you value so the wall is completed by the end of the lesson. Once completed, each participant may be eligible to take a small reward home for showing their teamwork.

As the group becomes familiar with this system it is fun to increase the difficulty of the build. To do this, nominate how many blocks must form the foundation before the build begins. Obviously, a foundation of just one block is notoriously difficult as the only way the blocks can go is up!

Continuing disruptive behaviours

Every so often, particularly when running smaller targeted groups, a child will display high level disruptive behaviours. This is always testing and detracts from the essence of what is trying to be achieved. At times simple circuit breakers prove successful; reminding everyone of the group rules, a facilitator calmly sitting next to the student, encouraging other students to help the student and so on.

When a student's disruptive behaviour has dominated a lesson, talk to them about it privately afterwards. Explain what the group needs from them. Set a simple goal together. Discuss exactly what they need to do to achieve the goal next time. It is also wise to recruit the advice and support of their parents.

If the difficulty persists facilitators do best by posing the following questions to themselves and making thoughtful decisions quickly. First, how long can the group sustain the barrage of negative behaviours? How much damage will result? Second, is the child genuinely up to this? Is the situation too free, too restrictive or too challenging for them? A compassionate decision may be to end the student's participation earlier rather than persevere. If this decision is required maintain an optimistic approach and offer the student the option of returning in a subsequent group.

Observation and feedback to parents

One of the most enlightening aspects of facilitating a social skilling group is the unique opportunity to talk, listen, share ideas, observe and truly get to know each of the students. It places facilitators in an extraordinary position.

Parents are aware of this and often look for feedback. So, if conditions permit, build scope into your organisation to offer brief feedback after each lesson. We recommend inviting parents to a one-hour 'parents only' meeting in weeks 2 or 3 of the programme and again around week 15. This allows for information gathering early on (it is also a perfect forum to collect teacher, parent and student surveys) and for feedback towards the end of the programme.

Sometimes, over a period of weeks, you may begin to develop concerns about a participant. It may be, for example, that they are constantly beset by worried thinking, overactivity or sadness. Once your thoughts crystallise it is crucial to speak to school leadership (if the programme is running in a school) and sensitively to the child's parents. Parents need to know your concern and also need to know that pathways exist for their child to access professional support; a school counsellor, a school psychologist, an independent psychologist, a GP, a paediatrician, a psychiatrist, a social worker or someone linked to a local community health centre.

Occasionally facilitators receive information from a child that is highly contentious or illicit. In such circumstances commit to following the protocol required by the school system or the system you work within. Our experience has shown that in rare instances when a facilitator has had to responsibly share sensitive information with appropriate personnel, or made a mandatory notification, the outcome has been helpful. The overriding motive is to deal with the issue compassionately and highly constructively.

Folders

Provide each group member with an A4-sized folder to transport lesson notes and incidentals to and from sessions. From time to time we encourage students to decorate their folders as this seems to heighten their attachment to the folder and boost the likelihood of it returning each week. Decorations range from line drawings and comic strips to collages, and always reflect a social theme.

In some instances folders do not return regularly. To avoid this becoming a source of annoyance have a supply of inexpensive A4-sized envelopes to send the notes home in, and be prepared to supply new ones each week.

Skill generalisation

To be honest, the effectiveness of generalising new social thinking and skills into real life settings by participants is variable; it has to be viewed as a notable challenge for most. This should be shared openly and candidly with parents right from the start.

Every group member is reliant on ongoing guidance and prompts from thoughtful adults; social thinking does not come naturally for most of the students who are the focus of this programme. Equally, it is unrealistic to expect a child who is under daily emotional or social duress at school to quickly incorporate the concepts learned in sessions into their everyday life. Evidence of social learning is usually gradual, and always generalises best within nurturing home and school environments (Verduyn, *et al.*, 1990).

Photocopiable resources now follow, and don't forget the online resources at www.whatsthebuzz.net.au!

What's the Buzz?
Group rules

Friendly words

Gentle actions

Quiet listening

Try your best

What's the Buzz?

Group rules feedback cards

What's the Buzz? Group rule feedback **Friendly words** 	***What's the Buzz?*** Group rule feedback **Gentle actions** 	***What's the Buzz?*** Group rule feedback **Quiet listening** 	***What's the Buzz?*** Group rule feedback **Try your best** 
What's the Buzz? Group rule feedback **Friendly words** 	***What's the Buzz?*** Group rule feedback **Gentle actions** 	***What's the Buzz?*** Group rule feedback **Quiet listening** 	***What's the Buzz?*** Group rule feedback **Try your best** 
What's the Buzz? Group rule feedback **Friendly words** 	***What's the Buzz?*** Group rule feedback **Gentle actions** 	***What's the Buzz?*** Group rule feedback **Quiet listening** 	***What's the Buzz?*** Group rule feedback **Try your best** 
What's the Buzz? Group rule feedback **Friendly words** 	***What's the Buzz?*** Group rule feedback **Gentle actions** 	***What's the Buzz?*** Group rule feedback **Quiet listening** 	***What's the Buzz?*** Group rule feedback **Try your best** 

What's the Buzz?

Thumbs up feedback cards

What's the Buzz?

Thumbs up!

What's the Buzz?

Thumbs up!

What's the Buzz?

Thumbs up!

What's the Buzz?

Thumbs up!

What's the Buzz?

Thumbs up!

What's the Buzz?

Thumbs up!

What's the Buzz?

Thumbs up!

What's the Buzz?

Thumbs up!

What's the Buzz?

Thumbs up!

What's the Buzz?

Thumbs up!

What's the Buzz?

Thumbs up!

What's the Buzz?

Thumbs up!

What's the Buzz?

Thumbs up!

Meeting People and Exiting

Explanation

From cross-cultural perspectives standard greetings certainly do vary! An acceptable greeting ranges from a light kiss on the cheek, to kisses on each cheek, hugging or back slapping, a modest wave of the hand, rubbing noses, bowing, curtsying or even poking tongues out at one another. Apparently, as part of the behavioural reforms in Victorian times, public kissing became socially improper. In its place a fashionable handshake emerged and quickly gained popularity. This kept men and women at a distance and helped avoid the old habit of kissing.

Within our own culture the idea of warmly greeting another appears straightforward at first. Yet, the truth is that a successful greeting contains a set of critical skills with the potential to engage another or instantly switch them off. It is not only shy or inexperienced young people who show difficulty with greeting others. We've all experienced meeting someone who does not engage eye contact, hangs their head, is stooped and offers little more than a mumble. This awkwardness is infectious and leaves both parties struggling for a positive greeting. On the other hand most of us have a memory of being enthusiastically greeted by a dominating handshake that continued for too long or actually hurt! Most can also recall a person who stood uncomfortably close and asked too many questions too quickly without seeming to care about the answers. Equally, there is an art to finish off an interaction and leave in a friendly way. Quite a few end their interactions abruptly, leaving their friend at a loss as to why they suddenly disappeared.

In reality, the skills required to successfully greet and farewell one another are intricate and crucial. This makes it worth spending time, in this lesson and at home, to explicitly teach children how to offer a friendly greeting and goodbye.

Materials required for Lesson 1

- Name tags

- Whiteboard/butcher's paper and a marker

- Post *What's the Buzz?* group rules (located on p. 20 in the photocopiable resources at the end of the previous chapter; alternatively, they can be downloaded from www.whatsthebuzz.net.au)

- Place an outline of the lesson on the whiteboard/butcher's paper

- Sets of coloured markers or pens for students to share

- Organise a folder or satchel for each group member so they are able to take things home

- One small soft ball for the game 'Greetings and Goodbyes'

- Eight small notebooks (or sheets of paper) and eight pencils for the game 'Greetings!'

- Organise the gold nuggets, cubes to build a friendship wall, group rule and reminder cards or a similar feedback device (see previous chapter)

- Organise a small gift or a reward token for each child

- Prepare handouts for parent(s):

  - One copy of this lesson for each parent to read

  - One copy of *After the Buzz: social thinking ideas for parents* for each parent to read (section follows this lesson).

Lesson 1

Arrange participants into a social circle and extend a warm welcome.

Hand out prepared name tags and discuss group rules together.

Display the gold nuggets, cubes to build a friendship wall, group rule and reminder cards or a similar feedback device to encourage positive social behaviours (see section on Practical Considerations). As you introduce the idea, and have the attention of students, pick up a gold nugget, a cube, a reminder card or similar to reinforce their cooperative spirit. Explain that if successful each student may leave with a small gift.

1. What's the Buzz?

What's the Buzz? introduces students to this lesson's topic and the new set of skills to be learned. A direct way to do this is to model the skills, either with a co-facilitator or a student volunteer. Stand so group members can watch and listen.

Steps to greet

Move close to the person

Stand about an arm's length away from the person, otherwise we enter their personal space and this can be uncomfortable for them.

Smile

Point to the smile on your face. A pleasant smile tells them that friendship is invited.

Look at them

While it is best to look at the eyes of another some feel uncomfortable doing this. Instead, look at the person's nose mouth or forehead. It works just as well!

Speak

Demonstrate the difference between a weak 'hello', a grumpy, cross or angry hello and a warm one that seeks engagement. If you know them, use the person's name. Wait for them to return your greeting. They may respond with a smile or a wave, or they may start talking. Be prepared to respond.

(Write the 'Steps to greet' – bold print only – on the whiteboard or butcher's paper)

Steps to receive a greeting

Ask a volunteer to greet you and model how to receive a greeting.

Look at them and smile

Point to your eyes and smile. Mention that as we look and smile the other person knows we wish to be friendly.

Move closer

By moving a little closer your body gives the message you want to accept their greeting.

Speak

Return the greeting by saying, 'hi' or 'hello'. Show the difference between an indifferent 'hi' and one that shows the person greeting that they are welcomed. Use the person's name if you know them. Now say something to help a conversation begin. One easy way is to ask a question:

- How are you going?
- What have you been up to?
- What do you want to do?
- What do you think about . . .?
- What did you watch on TV last night?
- What are you doing at the weekend?

(Write the 'Steps to receive a greeting'– bold print only – on the whiteboard or butcher's paper)

Steps to say goodbye (exiting)

Say goodbye when you leave or plan to do something else

Never just walk away. That's rude and leaves others feeling confused or upset.

Make it a friendly goodbye

Say something like 'bye', or 'I've got to go' or 'see you later.' Look at them while you say this.

Handshakes and hugs

With friends a handshake or a hug is not usually needed, but it can be important when saying goodbye to trusted familiar adults.

(Write the 'Steps to say goodbye' – bold print only – on the whiteboard or butcher's paper)

2. Show me the Buzz

Show me the Buzz gives students the opportunity to practise and show they understand the new skill set.

1   Help students to form pairs.

2   Each pair is to create a simple role-play showing a friendly greeting, a warm response to a greeting and a pleasant goodbye.

3   Draw their attention to the whiteboard or butcher's paper where the steps 'to greet', 'to receive a greeting' and 'to say goodbye' are written.

4   Give students a few minutes to rehearse.

5   Each pair performs in front of the group.

6   Encourage others to give constructive feedback.

3. Do you know the Buzz?

Do you know the Buzz? is a fast-moving question time. Its purpose is to consolidate the essence of the lesson. Arrange the group into a social circle. Ask them to listen carefully as they hear a series of rapid-fire statements. Their challenge is to decide whether the statement is true or false. If they believe a statement is true they are to put their thumbs up. If they think it is false they are to put their thumbs down. If they are not sure or want to challenge the statement they place both thumbs on the side.

Round 1

A good way to greet is to:

- smile

- say their name

- say 'hi' or 'hello'

- stare at their eyes

- get close to them

- make them giggle

- use a friendly sounding voice

- tell them all about yourself.

A good way to farewell is to:

- poke them with your finger

- give them a big hug

- just walk away

- yawn so they know you are bored and want to go

- look down at the ground and say, 'I've got to go now!'

- smile as you say, 'I've got to go now. See you later!'

- give them a handshake.

Round 2

Here are five questions about the greeting and exiting process.

Ask students to put their hands up and give the best answer they can!

Question 1: Tell me a phrase you might use to say goodbye?

Question 2: How could you greet a person without speaking?

Question 3: Why is it a good idea to warmly greet people?

Question 4: Why is it a good idea to say goodbye to people?

Question 5: Tell me one thing you could do a little more from now on when you greet or say goodbye to someone?

4. The Buzz

During *The Buzz* students play games that help strengthen the skills central to the lesson. The more group members are encouraged to play these, and similar games, the more opportunity they have to generalise their social thinking and social skills into their day-to-day interactions. Choose a game or two that match the maturity and interest of your group.

Back to Back (exciting for all ages)

This game can be played inside or outside. Players walk freely about a large space, but one of the players is nominated as 'it'. When 'it' calls, 'Back to back!' all players quickly find a partner and stand back to back. Then, 'it' says 'go' and players are free to move again. When 'it' calls 'Face to Face!' all players quickly find a partner, face each other, say 'hello' and shake hands.

Tell the players to be careful because 'it' will try to get with a partner during the change. The player left out will become 'it'. The idea is NOT to become 'it'.

Name Train (exciting for younger students)

Arrange the players so they are standing in a large circle. You begin by shuffling like a train across the circle making steam train sounds; have fun and exaggerate!

Eventually, come to a stop facing one of the players in the circle. Look at them and say, 'Hi, my name is, [your name] the Tank Engine'. The person facing you responds with, 'Hi, [they use your name], my name is [let's say their name is Mika]. You raise one arm high and then the other saying, 'Mika . . . Mika . . . Mika . . . Mika . . . Mika . . . Mika . . .'. You place Mika in front of you holding his waist. Mika pulls away from the station with you in tow. Both shuffle across the circle making steam train sounds. The steam train journey continues until everyone from the circle has joined the train and led the group!

Greetings and Goodbyes (passive for younger students)

Arrange the group into a circle. Explain that everyone will have the chance to roll the ball to someone as well as receive it. As participants roll the ball they give a friendly greeting to the person who receives it (being sure to use their name). As the ball is received the participant gives a friendly thank you (always using the name of the person who rolled the ball). The game continues until everyone has had a turn. Start by demonstrating the idea.

Greetings! (passive for older students)

As this is an old favourite it is best to set a five minute time limit. Players will require space to move about and must carry a pencil and small notebook (or sheet of paper) to record ideas. On 'go' students walk about and use friendly greetings as they pass one another; a thumbs up, a double thumbs up, a wink, a 'hello', a high five, a smile, a 'hi', a bow, blowing a kiss, a little wave, a 'how are you today?', a long wave and so on. The person being greeted must respond in a friendly way.

As the game progresses encourage participants to drop to the floor and add a new way to greet to their list. They may use their own ideas as well as collecting ideas they observe from others. The aim is to develop the longest possible list of friendly greetings within the time limit.

Once the time limit is reached move students back into the social circle. Move from student to student asking them to give one friendly greeting idea and show how it is done. Continue to do this until all ideas are exhausted. Ask students to add up the ideas on their list. Find out who has the most!

5. Goodbye Buzz

Bid students a warm goodbye and remind them to take their folders, which contain:

- a copy of this lesson for parents

- a copy of *After the Buzz: social thinking ideas for parents*.

As feedback for thoughtful behaviours each student may leave with a small gift.

After the Buzz: social thinking ideas for parents

Lesson 1: Meeting People and Exiting

This section highlights the value of parental care and that no one knows a child as well as a parent. The focus of Lesson 1 was to teach students how to greet, receive a greeting and say goodbye. These can be awkward skills for some and by explicitly teaching them we offer children a design to initiate improved social communication. Here are a few practical ideas parents can do at home to support the quality of their child's social thinking, especially with a view to strengthening their greeting and exiting skills.

- What do your children see?

  How do you greet and say goodbye? What are you showing your child? If you are certain that you greet and farewell warmly, then do not underestimate the influence you will have on them in the longer term, especially with a little purposeful guidance.

- Be encouraging

  Talk to your children about the importance of a warm greeting. It is more likely to lead to conversation and friendship. If your child feels shy about greeting people share the fact that many others feel exactly the same. Encourage them to try, even if it means taking on one small challenge at a time.

- Mental rehearsal

  As you are on the way to visit someone help your child to rehearse by discussing who will be at the gathering, what is likely to happen and what they should say as they enter. You might tell your child, 'Say hello to each person. If they say hello first then make sure you say hello back to them with that gorgeous smile of yours.' Also remind them that when it is time to leave it is important for them to do the same as you and say goodbye.

- The secret signal

  Prompt your child to remember the steps to greet and farewell by using an agreed secret signal. It may be as simple as saying, 'Sophie, have you got a tissue?' Alternatively, you might lightly squeeze their hand or ruffle their hair as a prompt that means, 'remember to greet or say goodbye to this person'. And, when they respond positively by using their skills, commend them! Good instruction and praise, in the company of patience, is the most valuable behaviour–shaping tool.

- Shaking hands

For boys and men in particular the handshake is often a part of the greeting process. Children are always fascinated by the stories surrounding its beginning. Share these stories with your child as a means to raise the importance of getting the handshake right. Although historical accounts are a little contradictory, the most popular story is that years and years ago a person showed an open right hand as proof they were not carrying a weapon. If two men met and displayed empty right hands, this seemingly meant a basic level of trust existed and that neither would reach for a weapon to stab the other. One variation to this story is that the handshake evolved to check for hidden knives. Apparently, the shaking motion of the hands and arms was supposed to displace any sharp objects that may have been kept in the sleeve. Share this brief history of handshaking with your child and teach them how to get their handshaking just right.

- Practice makes perfect

The safest place for your child to sharpen their greeting and goodbye skills is at home with family members. Make a start by expecting everyone to use them. As you see their confidence growing, also expect these skills to be used at school, cubs, ballet, karate, bowling club, scouts etc. This process is called training to proficiency, and can be used to reshape all sorts of behaviours. As an incentive for your child to continue using these skills create a chart and place a sticker or tick on it, and reward them for applying this to their life. Use it over several weeks until the skill is embedded.

After the Buzz . . . Lesson 1

Getting Attention

Explanation

Teachers and parents often talk about students with social skill difficulties as demanding or attention seeking. Let's be honest though, we all need attention. Getting attention from others reflects the way in which human beings are innately wired. We seek attention to create stimulation and make connections with others.

Students with developing social thinking and embryonic social skills are inclined to misread and mistime social interactions. They develop a style they think works for them. They think that what they do helps them to make connections, belong and fit in. In fact, without specific instruction and meaningful support they hone clumsy social habits that are interpreted by others as demanding, annoying, even downright strange. These young individuals genuinely struggle to grab attention using friendly behaviours.

In contrast, those with well developed social insight know how to hone pro-social behaviours. Their functioning allows them to gauge another's mood or response and get their timing just right. They quickly understand how they affect others and develop a consciousness that what they say and do actually influences the very core of every relationship they enter. Quickly they discover ways to get attention that satisfy themselves and others within the context of building a relationship.

The aim of this lesson is to examine how to get attention through the use of friendly behaviours. As students gradually experiment with their style of getting attention, the scope for more satisfying and successful communication begins.

Materials required for Lesson 2

- Name tags

- Whiteboard/butcher's paper and a marker

- Post *What's the Buzz?* group rules (located on p. 20; alternatively, they can be downloaded from www.whatsthebuzz.net.au)

- Place an outline of the lesson on the whiteboard/butcher's paper

- One bunch of keys and a blindfold for the game 'Sleeping Pirate'

- Organise the gold nuggets, cubes to build a friendship wall, group rule and reminder cards or a similar feedback device (see the chapter, Practical Considerations)

- Organise a small gift or a reward token for each child

- Prepare handouts for parent(s):

    - One copy of this lesson for each parent to read

    - One copy of *After the Buzz: social thinking ideas for parents* for each parent to read (section follows this lesson).

Lesson 2

Arrange participants into a social circle. Welcome them.

Ask who can remember the names of each group member. Prompt and support each student to try. Hand out prepared name tags.

Draw everyone's attention to the group rules. Display the gold nuggets, cubes to build a friendship wall, group rule and reminder cards or a similar motivational device to encourage positive social behaviours (see section on feedback ideas in the chapter, Practical Considerations). As you introduce the idea, and have the attention of students, pick up a gold nugget, a cube, a reminder card or similar to reinforce their cooperative spirit. Explain that if successful each student may leave with a small gift.

1. What's the Buzz?

What's the Buzz? introduces students to this lesson's topic and the new set of skills to be learned. Begin by explaining that wanting attention is normal.

There are two types of behaviours people use to get it:

1 Friendly behaviours – behaviours that look kind, caring and helpful to others

2 Demanding behaviours – behaviours that are seen by others as unhelpful, unfriendly, annoying and selfish.

How to get attention using friendly behaviours

*   Timing – look and listen so you know it is the right time to get the attention of another.

*   Use a smile and make contact with your eyes as you speak.

*   Once you speak or ask a question stop talking and listen to them.

*   Use friendly words and a friendly voice.

*   Put your body in a friendly position.

*   Offer to help.

*   Do what you have been asked to do by a trusted adult, even if it is not what you prefer.

*   Be fair.

*   Be truthful.

(Write the 'How to get attention using friendly behaviours' checklist on the whiteboard or butcher's paper)

How to get attention using demanding behaviours

- Look angry.

- Be bossy, threaten, tease or bully.

- Put others down.

- Talk too much or too loud.

- Interrupt.

- Tell lies, brag or show off.

- Get huffy because you can't have your way.

- Only talk about things that you want to talk about.

- Stand too close to people.

- Act silly.

- Refuse to help.

(Write the 'How to get attention using demanding behaviours' checklist on the whiteboard or butcher's paper)

2. Show me the Buzz

Show me the Buzz gives students the opportunity to practise and show they understand the new skill set.

Help students form pairs or small groups. Ask them to create a small role-play based on the behaviours within the 'How to get attention using friendly behaviours' checklist or 'How to get attention using demanding behaviours' checklist. Give participants five minutes to prepare their skits before showing the group.

Possible scenarios:

- Waiting to get back into a game, but it's taking too long!

- Needing a teacher's help with work in class

- Wanting Mum's attention while she's speaking on the phone

- Desperately wanting to go over to a friend's house, but Mum or Dad don't seem to care

- Joining a group at recess time and being keen to tell them what you did over the weekend.

Watch, enjoy and discuss each skit.

3. Do you know the Buzz?

Do you know the Buzz? is a fast-moving question time to clarify the ideas around the new set of skills for this lesson. Arrange group members into a social circle and encourage everyone to have a go. Here is the challenge!

Group quiz

- I want each of you to tell me one helpful attention seeking skill.

- Tell me one way to make sure your parents feel that you are hard to get along with.

- What is a good way to get attention from friends so they stay your friends?

- Tell me one sure way to seek attention from kids so they will NOT like you.

- There's an old wise saying, 'You reap what you sow'. What might this mean when it comes to seeking the attention of others?

4. The Buzz

The Buzz offers students a chance to play lively games to strengthen the ideas being developed. The emphasis in this lesson, and in these games, is leading students towards finding the very best ways to get attention from others.

Fighting for Attention (exciting for all ages)

Select two players. Ask them to stand up, move to the front of the group and position themselves either side of you.

These players will be asked to talk about a topic for thirty seconds in front of the group, but, they must talk 'at' you, 'non-stop,' using many of the characteristics from the 'How to get attention using demanding behaviours' checklist. Your response while they do this is one of disapproval; you stand stony faced with arms folded, looking at your watch.

Once they have finished, ask the audience to score their performances by holding up fingers on one hand. Five fingers up would indicate a superb performance. Add up the scores to determine a winner. Continue until everyone has a turn.

Wild Animals (exciting for all ages)

Whisper the name of an animal to each participant. For a group of four give two players the same animal name, and in a group of eight give two pairs the same name – everyone else has a different animal name. Once the name is given players are not permitted to speak or tell what animal they are. Instead, on 'go' each person makes the sound and movement of the animal they have been given while they move about. As soon as they find the same animal as themselves they sit on the floor together. Once all players are convinced they either have a partner or there isn't one, stop the game and ask each player to tell which animal they are. Children enjoy playing this game over and over!

Two Truths, One Lie (passive for older students)

This is an ideal introductory game as it offers a way for students to give a little information away about themselves, and to learn more about others. Explain that each of them will be given a turn to state two things that are true about themselves and one thing that is a lie. Each of the three statements should be confidently delivered. The rest of the group will try to guess which statement is the lie. Guessing the lie is the aim of the game! The best idea is for an adult to begin so they can model how it is done.

Sleeping Pirate (passive for younger students)

All players, except the sleeping pirate, sit in a circle on the floor. The sleeping pirate is blindfolded and sits cross-legged in the middle of the circle guarding a large bunch of keys on the floor nearby. Silently choose a child to creep up and ever so quietly take the rattling keys away from the pirate. Once they have the keys they attempt to return to their place in the circle and place the keys on the floor behind their back without the pirate hearing anything at all. The sleeping pirate listens intently, but says nothing.

Finally, the sleeping pirate is asked to remove their blindfold and have two or three attempts to guess the raider (number of guesses depends on the size of the group).

5. Goodbye Buzz

Bid students a warm goodbye and remind them to take their folders, which contain:

- a copy of this lesson for parents

- a copy of *After the Buzz: social thinking ideas for parents.*

As feedback for thoughtful behaviours each student may leave with a small gift.

After the Buzz: social thinking ideas for parents

Lesson 2: Getting Attention

In this lesson we examined how to get attention by using quality behaviours because children with poor social thinking are inclined to misread and mistime social interactions. They struggle to discriminate between seeking attention using friendly behaviours and grabbing it in ways that are experienced by others as off-putting. As children are led to experiment with varying styles of getting attention, the scope for more satisfying communication begins.

Here are a few ideas you may wish to draw on to support the way in which your child goes about gaining attention from others:

- Keep the big picture in mind

Sometimes when parents have long been absorbed in their child's tricky attention seeking behaviours, their optimism and patience become frayed. It is natural for parents to hit low spots or feel disheartened at times. What is effective is to keep the big picture in mind; progress is slower for some and it is the simple, day to day things we consistently say and do that makes the greatest difference for our children.

- The power to turn others 'on' and 'off'

Promote the idea that we cannot control the behaviour of others, but we can manage our actions and responses. Assist your child to understand that as they learn to seek attention by using friendly approaches others (adults and children) will be influenced to like them.

- People watching

A wonderful idea is to head off on an observational trip to watch people. First decide on the place to visit. As an example, you might head to a busy café with your child. Order a milkshake for them and a coffee for yourself and sit together at a table located near the counter. Take out a small sheet of paper and divide it into two columns. Write 'friendly behaviours' (great attention seeking skills) on one side and 'unhelpful behaviours' (demanding attention seeking) on the other. Keep a tally of people's personal style as they speak with the shop assistants. Record a word or a phrase in the appropriate column that describes what each person did to be friendly or otherwise. Study how they present themselves; the words they use, voice tone, patience, eye contact, body language, whether or not they smiled and how they gained attention if they had to wait. Watching people is enlightening! It provides direct modelling and the basis for a very productive discussion.

- 'How did they make you feel?'

  After you have met a friendly or unfriendly person, and your child has been with you, ask them how they felt in that person's company. Share with them how you felt. Ask whether that person's approach made them feel as though they wanted to be with them.

- Catch the friendly behaviours

  Many children who seek attention in negative ways do so because they believe it works for them. It's become their habit! They are reliant on perceptive adults to cue them towards more pro-social approaches. Be persistent and continue to talk about the best behaviours to gain quality attention.

  The golden rule is to catch positive behaviours and comment on them. This is the best way to develop the behaviours we want. To do this, one family decided to use raffle tickets to keep demanding attention seeking behaviours in check. They supplied their children with ten raffle tickets each at the beginning of a Saturday or Sunday. The idea was that each time one of their children blurted out demanding attention seeking requests such as: 'I want . . .', 'I need . . .', 'Can I have . . .', 'Can we go . . .', 'Can you do. . .', 'Where is . . .', 'You should . . .', 'Why can't I . . .', 'When will . . .', they had to hand over a raffle ticket before rephrasing their question in a friendly way. Those who had seven raffle tickets or more remaining by the end of the afternoon traded them in for a prearranged treat! It's not foolproof, but it took each of the children closer to appreciating how to seek attention with greater skill. Never forget that a little bit of clever tactical ignoring can go a long way too!

- Go gently, gently

  Remember that for children to experiment with new ideas, skills and behaviours they need to feel comfortable and relaxed within the family. Be gentle and consistent with your child when attempting to change old habits. So often a behaviour that appears as aloof, too highly spirited or unfriendly is more a measure of their awkward social thinking.

After the Buzz . . . Lesson 2

Following Instructions

Explanation

Efficiently following instructions is elusive for many children. However, take a moment to reflect because there is much more to following an instruction than first meets the eye. To do this successfully an individual needs to be aware of what has been asked. That's right, it all starts in the looking and listening, and many of the children who are the focus of this group struggle with observing and listening. They live with highly distractible and egocentric traits, let alone social clumsiness, expressive language problems or elevated levels of anxiousness. They do not possess the natural temperament to look, listen, integrate ideas, comply, remember and persevere.

In addition, many struggle with the act of breaking away from what is important to them. Their style is to think and do it their way. They are so intent on having their own needs met that it is hard for them to break set and raise the empathy required to meet the needs of others. Quite a few will say, 'Why, what's the point?' or worse, 'No, that's stupid!' simply because they do not see the purpose or have an interest in what is being asked. Their personal inflexibility confines them to what they know and are interested in. Unless there is an obvious reason to oblige, cooperation is genuinely tricky. This inflexible style of thinking reduces their capacity to stop a task on command and smoothly move to a new one. Yet, an individual's capacity to freely switch from one task to another is a foundation stone of personal success and heavily relied on by teachers and parents.

Do not underestimate the intricate interplay of complex skills necessary to successfully follow directions. This skill set requires the sophisticated integration of looking, listening, compliance, remembering, empathy and persistence capacities. Developmentally, it can take much longer for some children to become fluent in this area.

In the meantime, they are dependent on recurring explicit training that, over time, supports them to follow instructions and directions despite not having a strong desire to do so.

The aim of this lesson is to set in motion the participants' interest and desire to follow directions, and to skill parents and educators in constructive approaches to do this.

Materials required for Lesson 3

- Name tags

- Whiteboard/butcher's paper and marker

- Post *What's the Buzz?* group rules (located on p. 20; alternatively, they can be downloaded from www.whatsthebuzz.net.au)

- Place an outline of the lesson on the whiteboard/butcher's paper

- Prepare 'Following instructions: role-play cards' (located in the photocopiable resources at the end of this lesson; alternatively, they can be downloaded from www.whatsthebuzz.net.au)

- One small notebook and pencil for each student

- Twelve large paper bags with a list of items to be found recorded on the front for the game 'Scavenger Hunt'

- Organise the gold nuggets, cubes to build a friendship wall, group rule and reminder cards or a similar feedback device (see the chapter, Practical Considerations)

- Organise a small gift or a reward token for each child

- Prepare handouts for parent(s):

  - One copy of this lesson for each parent to read

  - One copy of *After the Buzz: social thinking ideas for parents* for each parent to read (section follows this lesson).

Lesson 3

Arrange participants into a social circle. Welcome them. Once again assist students to recall the names of one another. Again, hand out the prepared name tags. Draw everyone's attention to the group rules. Display the feedback device to encourage positive social behaviours (see section on feedback ideas in the chapter, Practical Considerations). Explain that if successful each student may leave with a small gift.

1. What's the Buzz?

What's the Buzz? introduces students to this lesson's topic and the new set of skills to be learned. Explain that there are things we like to do and things that are not as much fun. For example, most people don't like or complain about the following:

- washing dishes

- tidying up

- packing things away

- making the bed

- taking out the garbage

- doing homework

- watching television programmes chosen by someone else

- helping someone with something that's boring or not much fun.

Ask the group whether they do some of these things. What do they do when they don't feel like doing what they have been asked? What do they do if they are too busy doing their own thing? What usually happens then?

5 reasons to follow instructions:

1   It shows that you are growing up. As adults see more cooperation they give children more freedom.

2   It is helpful. Helpfulness is what good relationships depend on.

3   When you follow instructions adults feel happier. When they are happy they are more willing to have fun.

4   It stops you from getting into trouble.

5   You will feel proud of yourself. Doing something you would prefer not to do will attract praise.

(Write the '5 reasons to follow instructions' checklist on the whiteboard/butcher's paper)

2. Show me the Buzz

Show me the Buzz gives students the opportunity to practise and show they understand the new skill set.

Form students into pairs and ask each pair to choose a 'Following instructions: role-play card'.

Each card contains one of the following role plays.

Following instructions: role-play 1

> One partner is a parent and the other is their child. The parent asks the child to tidy up the bedroom. The child agrees to do it, but asks if they can do it later because they are in the middle of a game. The parent praises the child's helpfulness and suggests a reward will be offered when they finish!

Following instructions: role-play 2

> One partner is a parent and the other is their child. The parent asks the child to tidy up the bedroom. The child complains because they want to keep playing their computer game. The parent says, 'I'm not arguing, either you do it, or go to bed an hour earlier tonight.' Show how the child could fix the problem and follow the instruction.

Following instructions: role-play 3

> One partner is a parent and the other is their child. The parent asks the child to start their homework. The child agrees, but asks if they could do it after the television programme is finished. The parent smiles and says, 'Sure, that's fine.'

Following instructions: role-play 4

> One partner is a teacher and the other is a student. The teacher asks the student to join a group they don't like very much. The student looks put out, folds their arms and says, 'It's not fair. You know I don't like them.' The teacher looks annoyed. Show how the student could fix the problem and follow the instruction.

Following instructions: role-play 5

> One partner is a parent and the other is their child. The family has just arrived home after a day at the beach. Everyone is tired. The parent asks the child to help unpack the car. The child doesn't want to and walks off. The parent looks annoyed and begins to follow the child. Show how the child could fix the problem and follow the instruction.

Following instructions: role-play 6

> One partner is a parent and the other is their child. Everyone has just arrived home after a day at the beach. The parent asks the child to help out. The child runs inside to feed the cat and dog. The parent sees the child running inside and calls out, 'Didn't you hear me? Get back here and help!' Show how the child could fix the problem and follow the instruction.

Following instructions: role-play 7

One partner is a parent and the other is their child. The parent calls out, 'Hey, Alice could you please put your homework in your bag and then get your lunch box and bring it to me!' The child keeps reading. The parent comes up to them with hands on hips and says, 'Did you hear what I said?' Show how the child could fix the problem and care.

Following instructions: role-play 8

One partner is a teacher and the other is a student. The student is asked to pick up the books at the end of the lesson. The student doesn't want to do it because everyone will be sorted into teams before they finish and they'll miss out. However, they want to be helpful. Show what the child could do so the teacher sees them as mature and caring.

Following instructions: role-play 9

One partner is a teacher and the other is a student. The student is sitting in class feeling bored. Suddenly the teacher asks them to do something and they have no idea what it is. They feel embarrassed. Show how the child could fix the problem and follow the instruction.

Give students a few minutes to practise before asking them to perform their role-play in front of the group. Enjoy the performances. Encourage participants to applaud and give positive, constructive feedback. Ask the students to compare the feelings they have between being respectful and helpful, and being difficult to get along with.

3. Do you know the Buzz?

Do you know the Buzz? is a quick question time to consolidate the concepts gathered in the lesson. Students are quizzed on ideas they have learned. Encourage everyone to have a go. Here is the challenge.

Round 1

Ask the group to listen carefully to the statements below. Their challenge is to decide whether the statement is true or false. If they believe a statement is true they are to put their thumbs up. If they think it is false they are to put their thumbs down. If they are not sure, think it's debatable, and they want to challenge the statement they are to place their thumbs to the side.

- Parents like doing jobs around the house so we don't need to help.

- Following instructions helps to keep us out of trouble.

- Looking at the person who is asking the instruction is respectful.

- If I ignore the instruction the person asking will eventually stop and I won't have to do it.

- When I'm not sure what to do I should ask for help.

- When we follow instructions we are more likely to get along with others.

- Following an instruction will make adults feel pleased.

- Listening to the person's voice as they give the instruction helps you work out how serious they are.

- If I'm not sure about an instruction I should cry or sulk.

- When we don't do what we've been asked to do we disappoint others.

- Follow every instruction you are given.

- Sometimes we just have to do things we don't like doing.

- When I follow instructions I give the impression that I'm a caring and helpful person.

Round 2

Arrange group members to sit with the partner they performed the role-play with earlier on. Cover the whiteboard and ask each pair to record the '5 reasons to follow instructions' into a notebook. Challenge them to remember as many as they can. Remind them to whisper so no one hears. Give students a few minutes. Then, ask them to return to the circle and tell what they have remembered.

4. The Buzz

During *The Buzz* students play games that strengthen the skills central to the lesson. The emphasis on today's games is for students to work cooperatively and follow instructions. Choose a game or two that match the maturity and interest of your group.

Scavenger Hunt (passive for all ages)

Scavenger Hunt is an outside game. It is wise to set boundaries. Help group members to find a partner. Each pair is given a paper bag and on it is a list of four, five or six items they must find together. They have just five minutes to get the best example of each. Here are a few ideas:

- a small twig

- a twig with two little branches coming off it

- a piece of bark

- a smooth round pebble

- a stone with two or more colours in it

- a long leaf

- a short, wide leaf

- a leaf with more than two points on it

- a flower

- a piece of paper

- something shiny

- something soft

- something rare

- something amazing

- something that is a part of something bigger

- something that used to be alive

- something that is alive and very small

- something really smooth

- something that looks alien.

It is fun to return to the social circle, look at what each pair decided to collect and hear them justify their decision.

Port and Starboard (exciting for all ages)

This listening game is best played in a large room. Responding to the commands below, students quickly perform the appropriate actions. Give the group a while to warm up, practise and remember the commands, then start removing the slowest players until only one or two are left.

- 'Port' – run to the left hand side of the area.

- 'Starboard' – run to right hand side of the area.

- 'Captain's coming aboard' – stand to attention, perfectly still and maintain a salute.

- 'Submarines' – lie on the floor as stiff as a board.

- 'Hoist the mainsail' – run vigorously on the spot with arms looking as though they are hoisting the rigging.

- 'Mess deck' – sit cross-legged on the floor gobbling lunch.

- 'Davey Jones' – lie on tummy or back with feet kicking wildly in the air.

- 'Up periscope' – stand up straight and hold both hands to eyes as if looking through a periscope.

Mr and Mrs Wright (exciting for all ages)

Have everyone stand well away from each other. Tell them that you are going to read a story about Mr and Mrs Wright and that they will need to listen very carefully. When they hear you say the word 'right' they will have to jump to the right. When they hear you say 'left' they will have to jump to the left. This game is a lot of fun, but each person's success hinges on them concentrating, listening and remembering. It's all about following directions to the letter!

The story . . .

This is a story about Mr and Mrs WRIGHT. One evening they were baking cookies. Mrs WRIGHT called from the kitchen, 'Oh, no, there is no flour LEFT! You will need to go out to the store RIGHT away.'

'I can't believe you forgot to check the pantry,' grumbled Mr WRIGHT. 'You never get anything RIGHT!'

'Don't be difficult, dear,' replied Mrs WRIGHT. 'You could have LEFT by now and been on your way. It will only take twenty minutes if you come RIGHT back. Go to the Post Office up on the main road, and turn LEFT at the stop sign. Then go past the fruit shop we usually go to, and turn RIGHT, and there it will be on your LEFT,' declared Mrs WRIGHT as her husband LEFT the house.

Mr WRIGHT found the store and asked the shop assistant where he could find the flour. The shop assistant pointed and said, 'Go to Aisle four and turn LEFT. The flour and sugar will be on your LEFT.'

Mr WRIGHT made his purchase and walked RIGHT out the door. He turned LEFT, but he couldn't remember where he had LEFT his car. Suddenly he remembered that he had driven Mrs WRIGHT'S car and that his car was in the driveway at home RIGHT where he had LEFT it. He finally found the RIGHT car and put his things RIGHT inside. Eventually, a weary Mr WRIGHT found his way home.

Mrs WRIGHT had been waiting impatiently. 'I thought you would be RIGHT back,' she said. 'I LEFT all the cookie ingredients on the kitchen counter, and the cats got into the milk. You'll just have to go RIGHT out again.'

Mr WRIGHT sighed. He had no energy LEFT. 'I am going RIGHT to bed,' he said. 'Anyway, I need to go on a diet, so I might as well start RIGHT now. Isn't that RIGHT, dear?'

Author unknown

Hot and Cold (passive for all ages)

This legendary game can be played inside or outside. If outside, commence by explaining the boundaries for students to stay within. Choose a location you wish students to arrive at. The idea is that you do not tell them the destination you have selected. They will need to listen to your instructions to find the point you have in mind. The only clues you will deliver are words such as: 'freezing', 'cold', 'warm', 'warmer', 'colder', 'hotter', 'really hot', 'boiling', 'cooler'. Your clues gradually drive the group to find the hottest spot. When they arrive let them know they have successfully listened and followed instructions. It is also great fun to divide the group in half. Have half watching while the others try to find the hottest spot as it's just as much fun to watch!

5. Goodbye Buzz

Bid students a warm goodbye and remind them to take their folders, which contain:

- a copy of this lesson for parents

- a copy of *After the Buzz: social thinking ideas for parents.*

As feedback for thoughtful behaviours each student may leave with a small gift.

After the Buzz: social thinking ideas for parents

Lesson 3: Following Instructions

In this lesson your child learned how to follow directions and what the benefits are. Here are a few tips for parents to improve their children's capacity to follow instructions.

- Learning how to look, listen and wait take time

  Do what you can to model the best listening and observing skills. For example, if your child wants your attention while you are busy let them know you will help them in a few minutes once you are finished. This shows respect and that you do care about what they want. It also models healthy communication, which helps to reduce stress!

- Strategies to strengthen looking and listening skills

  Every so often invent opportunities to brainstorm what good listening and looking actually look like. Watch others and highlight how they show essential looking and listening skills under the headings of: head, eyes, ears, face, voice, arms, hands, body. Display them on a checklist for everyone in the family to see.

  - Play listening games to identify animal or environmental sounds. Listen to readymade CDs to do this.

  - Have fun with musical instruments or get your children to copy clapping rhythms.

  - Playing a quick burst of 'Simple Simon' can raise looking and listening readiness. Build out the degree of complexity by using three and four instructions such as, clap your hands, click your fingers and stamp your feet.

  - Read to children. During the story, pause and ask questions to ensure they are tuned in and listening.

  - Play the good fun listening game: 'When I went to the shop . . . I bought some bread'. The next person says, 'When I went to the shop . . . I bought some bread and a pizza'. Then, the next repeats the previous items and then adds their own, and so the game builds.

  - As you deliver an important instruction hold up a visually impressive object to cue children into knowing that right now is a critical time to listen.

  - Count down from five to zero with children knowing that by the time you reach zero they need to be tuned in ready to look and listen.

  – When giving the instruction, get down on their level and make eye contact with your child.

  – If necessary, gently touch them on the arm so their attention turns to you.

  – Ask them to repeat the instruction.

• Give the instruction once

Most of us fall into the trap of repeating instructions because our children actually condition us to do it! In the event that they can't remember the instruction, and you must repeat it, use only key words, i.e. 'socks, undies, washing machine'.

• Chunk instructions

Break instructions into small parts, keeping them short and simple. As an example, one way to reduce conflict over bedroom tidying up is to chunk instructions. Try saying:

  – 'Put your shoes back into your cupboard before your TV show.'

  – 'Restack the books into your bookshelf. I'll help you start.'

  – 'I want you to tidy your top drawer. Call me if you need some help.'

Chunking tasks helps to avoid overload, which so often leads to refusal or avoidance. Start small and be careful how you instruct your child to clean up their bedroom. *'Go and clean up your bedroom right now!'* is likely not to get the best result.

• Visual strategies

A visual strategy is virtually any visual way to support someone's understanding about what to do, when to do it and how to do it; schedules, timetables, planners, stamps, charts, posters, post–it stickers with reminders, a text message, picture prompts, PowerPoint presentation, dot point instructions, lists, checklists, tick lists, calendars, the same silly smile, notes, signs, messages, cue cards and even a string tied to a finger. These are all visual strategies and the only limitation is our imagination! They are truly invaluable. Whatever you decide to trial set it up with your child and use it every day!

Well developed visual strategies provide children with a permanent and personalised way to improve social and organisational skills. They are brilliant little anxiety savers because they give reassurance about how a desired behaviour, routine or skill should be tackled. Children can carry their visual helpers with them in the forms of business cards, key tags and wallets. For greater security they can even attach them to lanyards and wear them.

• Praise!

Always praise children for listening and responding well. Praise is the most effective shaper of behaviour!

• Practice makes perfect

Work with your child to help them practise following an instruction each day. Try some of the ideas presented below. The best idea is to head into this wanting to make it successful and build their skills.

- Place the clothes in the washing machine and turn it on.

- Hang out the clothes to dry.

- Put the wet clothes in the dryer and turn it on.

- Iron a few carefully selected items.

- Load the dishwasher.

- Wash the dishes.

- Dry the dishes.

- Pack the dishes away.

- Start homework when asked.

- Vacuum, sweep or mop the floor of a room.

- Help wash the car.

- Tidy up a mess somewhere.

- Clean a window.

- Tidy up the bedroom.

- Make a bed.

- Tidy up the playroom.

- Take out the garbage.

Photocopiable resources now follow, and don't forget the online resources at www.whatsthebuzz.net.au!

What's the Buzz

Following instructions: role-play cards

What's the Buzz?   Following instructions: role-play 1

One partner is a parent and the other is their child. The parent asks the child to tidy up the bedroom. The child agrees to do it, but asks if they can do it later because they are in the middle of a game. The parent praises the child's helpfulness and suggests a reward will be offered when they finish!

Focus: cooperation and clear communication

What's the Buzz?   Following instructions: role-play 2

One partner is a parent and the other is their child. The parent asks the child to tidy up the bedroom. The child complains because they want to keep playing their computer game. The parent says, 'I'm not arguing, either you do it, or go to bed an hour earlier tonight.' Show how the child could fix the problem and follow the instruction.

Focus: a negative response

What's the Buzz?   Following instructions: role-play 3

One partner is a parent and the other is their child. The parent asks the child to start their homework. The child agrees, but asks if they could do it after the television programme is finished. The parent smiles and says, 'Sure, that's fine.'

Focus: cooperation and clear communication

What's the Buzz

Following instructions: role-play cards *continued . . .*

What's the Buzz?   Following instructions: role-play 4

One partner is a teacher and the other is a student. The teacher asks the student to join a group they don't like very much. The student looks put out, folds their arms and says, 'It's not fair. You know I don't like them.' The teacher looks annoyed. Show how the student could fix the problem and follow the instruction.

Focus: think first

What's the Buzz?   Following instructions: role-play 5

One partner is a parent and the other is their child. The family has just arrived home after a day at the beach. Everyone is tired. The parent asks the child to help unpack the car. The child doesn't want to and walks off. The parent looks annoyed and begins to follow the child. Show how the child could fix the problem and follow the instruction.

Focus: ignoring an instruction

What's the Buzz?   Following instructions: role-play 6

One partner is a parent and the other is their child. Everyone has just arrived home after a day at the beach. The parent asks the child to help out. The child runs inside to feed the cat and dog. The parent sees the child running inside and calls out, 'Didn't you hear me? Get back here and help!' Show how the child could fix the problem and follow the instruction.

Focus: poor communication

What's the Buzz

Following instructions: role-play cards *continued . . .*

What's the Buzz?   **Following instructions: role-play 7**

One partner is a parent and the other is their child. The parent calls out, 'Hey, Alice could you please put your homework in your bag and then get your lunch box and bring it to me!' The child keeps reading. The parent comes up to them with hands on hips and says, 'Did you hear what I said?' Show how the child could fix the problem and care.

Focus: ignoring an instruction

What's the Buzz?   **Following instructions: role-play 8**

One partner is a teacher and the other is a student. The student is asked to pick up the books at the end of the lesson. The student doesn't want to do it because everyone will be sorted into teams before they finish and they'll miss out. However, they want to be helpful. Show what the child could do so the teacher sees them as mature and caring.

Focus: positive problem solving

What's the Buzz?   **Following instructions: role-play 9**

One partner is a teacher and the other is a student. The student is sitting in class feeling bored. Suddenly the teacher asks them to do something and they have no idea what it is. They feel embarrassed. Show how the child could fix the problem and follow the instruction.

Focus: positive problem solving

Being Friendly

Explanation

Children who are the focus of *What's the Buzz?* often struggle to use friendly behaviours, and instead put others off. Some find it difficult to be patient, listen and to accept the opinions of others, and when things don't work out for them their emotions overwhelm them and rapidly spin out of control. In contrast are those who are deeply shy and worry. Initiating, let alone maintaining a relationship, is painfully daunting. To survive the highly dynamic social rigours at school these children spend play times sitting on a bench intently reading. Unfortunately, this survival styled behaviour attracts everyone's attention and earns them unkind comments and labels.

At home, when someone arrives to play, parents also witness their child's frail social skills. They watch their son or daughter become overexcited or stage struck. Pauses in conversations develop and the two lost souls wander aimlessly about the house looking for something to do. In desperation, they boot up the computer to play a game. After a few minutes their child has the controls and is completely absorbed by the game. Within a few minutes the friend has disengaged and the idea of having a friend over to build a relationship has soured. Interestingly, many children with social skill difficulties are aware of their limitations, and anxiousness about their performance is never too far away.

This lesson highlights the skills required so others see us as being friendly.

It begins with a few facts about body language. The way we sit, stand, lean, employ eye contact, use facial expressions and the tone of our voice transmits critical messages about us to others. For example, simple things such as sitting up and leaning slightly forward while listening is interpreted by others as being interested in what they are saying and works in one's favour when communicating. Alternatively, mumbling, avoiding eye contact and looking towards the floor shows insecurity or a lack of interest. Knowing how to use positive body language, friendly voices and engaging feedback provides every human being with a relational edge. When we teach simple, friendly behaviours to children, and they begin to trial them, they start to look more at ease and more approachable to peers. This translates to peers seeing them as more inviting to be with and feeling more inclined to socialise with them. As this type of interaction gently rises opportunities to develop stronger relationships and more complex social skills gradually unfold.

Materials required for Lesson 4

- Whiteboard/butcher's paper and marker

- Post *What's the Buzz?* group rules (located on p. 20; alternatively, they can be downloaded from www.whatsthebuzz.net.au)

- Place an outline of the lesson on the whiteboard/butcher's paper

- Prepare 'Guess what? Friendly or unfriendly role-play cards' (located in the photocopiable resources at the end of this lesson; alternatively, they can be downloaded from www.whatsthebuzz.net.au)

- Photocopy and enlarge the selection of images for 'Who's being friendly?' (located in the photocopiable resources at the end of this lesson; alternatively, they can be downloaded from www.whatsthebuzz.net.au)

- Organise the gold nuggets, cubes to build a friendship wall, group rule and reminder cards or a similar feedback device (see the chapter, Practical Considerations)

- Organise a small gift or a reward token for each child

- Prepare handouts for parent(s):

  - One copy of this lesson for each parent to read
  - One copy of *After the Buzz: social thinking ideas for parents* for each parent to read (section follows this lesson).

Lesson 4

Arrange participants into a social circle. Welcome them. Draw everyone's attention to the group rules. Display the feedback device to encourage positive social behaviours (see section on feedback ideas in the chapter, Practical Considerations). Explain that if successful each student may leave with a small gift.

1. What's the Buzz?

What's the Buzz? introduces students to this lesson's topic and the new set of skills to be learned. Explain that every person needs to do three things in order to be seen as friendly. They need to present a friendly face, a friendly body and use a friendly voice tone. As soon as we do these things others quickly see us as wanting to be friendly.

Stand in front of the group and demonstrate how to be friendly:

A friendly face

- Soften your face so that it is easy to move.

- Make sure your eyebrows are smooth and relaxed, otherwise you might look worried or angry.

- Smile! A smile says that you are inviting friendship. Let's see you smile?

- Look at the person's eyes or face because this signals you are interested in them.

A friendly body

- Relax your body. Stand tall and open your chest by gently pulling your shoulders back.

- Keep your arms by your side. Folding your arms may give the idea that you are not interested and clenched fists might suggest you are ready for a fight!

- Stand about an arm's length away from the person. Standing too close will make them feel uncomfortable and standing too far away means they will not take you seriously.

Friendly words

- Include greetings such as: 'hi', 'hello', 'hey there'.

- Friendly words also include asking questions: 'how are you?', 'how was your weekend?', 'what did you do last night?'.

- And, when the time is right offer a compliment; 'it's great to see you' 'you're good at this' 'I like doing this with you' 'cool haircut'.

2. Show me the Buzz

Show me the Buzz gives students the opportunity to practise and show they understand the new skill set.

Hand one 'Guess what? Friendly or unfriendly role-play card' to each participant. The cards contain simple scenarios. Once students read their card ask them to place it face down on the floor. They may look at it later if they wish to. Explain that in a moment you want each person to act out the situation on the card to the group using the face, body and words suggested. Students can choose someone in the group to play a part alongside them. The group will try to guess whether they are being friendly or unfriendly.

Guess what? Friendly or unfriendly role-play card 1

You are happy to see a friend at school, so with a smile, a friendly voice and hands by your side you say, 'Hi, how are you today?' Ask the group to guess whether you were friendly or unfriendly. How could they tell?

Guess what? Friendly or unfriendly role-play card 2

You are really pleased to see a friend. You grab and shake them very hard saying, 'Hi, guess what I did last night? I've got lots to tell you.' Ask the group to guess whether you were friendly or unfriendly. How could they tell?

Guess what? Friendly or unfriendly role-play card 3

You walk up to someone and smile. You say, 'It's great to see you.' But, you fold your arms, use a flat voice and look at the floor. Ask the group to guess whether you were friendly or unfriendly. How could they tell?

Guess what? Friendly or unfriendly role-play card 4

You walk up to someone with a smile. You say, 'Do you want to do the same as yesterday? That was fun!' Use a voice that shows you like them. Keep good eye contact. Ask the group to guess whether you were friendly or unfriendly. How could they tell?

Guess what? Friendly or unfriendly role-play card 5

You rush up to someone. You are angry and have your fists clenched next to your chest. You shout, 'That wasn't fair. You cheated and you'll be sorry.' Ask the group to guess whether you were friendly or unfriendly. How could they tell?

Guess what? Friendly or unfriendly role-play card *6*

> You are pleased to see a friend. You rush up and hug them as you say, 'Hi, it's great to see you today?' Ask the group to guess whether you were friendly or unfriendly. How could they tell?

Guess what? Friendly or unfriendly role-play card *7*

> You walk up to someone. You are not pleased to see them. You do not smile. You do not look at their face. As you say, 'hello' you use a voice that says you don't care about them. Ask the group to guess whether you were friendly or unfriendly. How could they tell?

Guess what? Friendly or unfriendly role-play card *8*

> You are happy to see this person. Using a friendly voice you say, 'Great to see you!' But, you stand too close. Ask the group to guess whether you were friendly or unfriendly. How could they tell?

3. Do you know the Buzz?

Do you know the Buzz? is a lively question time. Students will be quizzed on ideas around the new set of skills within today's lesson. Encourage everyone to have a go.

Round 1

Arrange the group into a social circle and move quickly from student to student.

1   Tell me ONE way to make your face look friendly (possible answers: good eye contact, an inviting smile, relax forehead and eyebrows, relaxed face, look interested).

2   Tell me ONE way to make your voice sound friendly (possible answers: choose friendly words, use a light tone, laugh if it is appropriate, speak confidently).

3   Tell me ONE way to make your body look friendly (possible answers: relax your body, stand tall, open your shoulders, hands by your side, lean forward, look interested).

4   Tell me ONE way to make sure others see an unfriendly you (possible answers: look down, look away, shrug, fold arms, make fists, hug inappropriately, show a tense face, roll your eyes, say something mean, use a bored sounding voice).

Round 2: Who's being friendly?

Arrange the group so they can see the images you have downloaded onto your computer. Alternatively, use the images provided at the end of the lesson. Students must decide whether each person in the image looks friendly, unfriendly or something else! If they believe someone looks as though they are showing friendly behaviours they are to put their thumbs up. If they think the behaviour looks unfriendly they are to put their thumbs down. If they believe it is too hard to tell they are to put their thumbs to the side, and when challenged must be prepared to explain their decision.

4. The Buzz

During *The Buzz* students play games to help them practise their newly learned skills. The emphasis in *The Buzz* today is for students to show *being friendly* skills. Ask them how they can show these. Suggestions may include:

- Let someone else go first.

- Be encouraging by saying, 'good luck' 'well done' 'wow' 'unreal' 'unbelievable' 'too cool.'

- Be patient.

- Enjoy watching the others.

- Smile and laugh with the group.

- Try not to show your disappointment if you do not do well.

- The best idea is to play to win friends, not to only win the game.

'Yes' and 'No' (passive for all ages)

The aim of 'Yes' and 'No' is to honestly answer questions from the group without saying the words 'yes or 'no' and without nodding or shaking your head to indicate a 'yes' or 'no'. Have the person answering the questions sit in front of the group facing them. The first member of the group might ask, 'Are you a boy?' A clever answer could be, 'I'm sure I am!' or 'Of course not!' The next question goes to the next group member. As soon as the person facing the group says, 'yes' or 'no' or nods or shakes their head they are out and replaced by the person who asked the question. Just for fun, keep a tally of which person was able to field the most questions successfully.

Mixed-up Body Parts (passive for all ages)

For this game it is best to sit participants in a social circle.

Start off by pointing to your elbow and calling it 'foot'. Then, look at the group and ask, 'Do you see the idea?' Older groups will catch on fast, but for younger groups it may be wise to have a practice run around the circle first.

Once everyone is ready the game begins with each player taking a turn to touch a body part and deliberately naming it with another body part name. Each player must vary what they choose and has just five seconds to respond. Anyone who cannot respond in time is out. This certainly gives an insight into flexibility. Last player remaining wins!

Catching the Dragon's Tail (exciting for all ages)

Create a dragon by forming the group into a long line. Arrange the players so they have their hands on the shoulders of the player in front of them. The first in line is the dragon's head. The last in line is the dragon's tail; always keen to lash to the right and left to get away from the snapping head!

Players wait in a straight line and on 'go' the head runs around towards the tail trying to catch it. The dragon must move with the head and remain unbroken. If the body breaks the head becomes the tail and the next in line becomes the head, and the game is restarted. If the head catches the tail, they may continue to be the head or give their turn away to someone else.

5. Goodbye Buzz

Bid students a warm goodbye and remind them to take their folders, which contain:

- a copy of this lesson for parents

- a copy of *After the Buzz: social thinking ideas for parents*.

As feedback for thoughtful behaviours each student may leave with a small gift.

After the Buzz: social thinking ideas for parents

Lesson 4: Being Friendly

This section highlights that no one knows your child as well as you, and because of this, no one else has such a potent influence on them. In this lesson the skills required so others might see your child as friendly were explored. With this in mind, here are a few ideas to help your children practise and consolidate friendly styled behaviours.

- Play-dates

  Most parents yearn for their children to find happiness in having a friend over to play. However, it makes no sense to do this until quite short, highly structured, one-on-one play-dates run with consistent success. Keep in mind that younger children require greater adult direction. Nevertheless, strategic planning, beginning at the simplest level, makes smiles possible for everyone!

  Level one: at home after school

  Arrange something for your child and their friend to eat and drink. Direct them to watch a television programme or a short DVD and then take the friend home. A word to the wise: it may go against your grain to allow your child to watch too much television, but in this situation it takes the pressure off them to perform. In fact, the television programme is likely to be a catalyst for them to chat. Work on creating a short, structured and enjoyable play-date. Leave them both wanting more!

  Level two: off to the park

  Walk or drive your child and their friend to the shop. Buy something to eat and drink and visit a nearby park, bike park, skate park or playground for just thirty minutes. Then take the friend home. Again, keep the play-date short, structured and pleasantly memorable!

  Level three: a cook up

  Set up a visit so your child and their friend might cook something and eat the spoils afterwards. Then it's off home with the friend!

  Level four: at the shops

  Take your child and their friend to the local shopping centre. Depending on their age and independence, set them up with a drink and leave them to finish their drinks and do a little window shopping. Organise them to visit several stores they have an interest in and nominate a time and place to meet ready for you to drive the friend home.

Level five: venture a little further

Take your child and their friend to a place they are both likely to enjoy: the swimming pool, the beach, a climb on the rocks, tadpoling, frog hunting, or some time at the bike track – anything that structures activity. Pack a snack or lunch, and be sure to tell them their play has to be brief – it's surprising how quickly so many interesting things can be found when time is at a premium!

Level six: an evening dinner and a DVD

This structured approach guarantees a win for all. Manipulate the situation so that the experience is an enjoyable experience. This may mean arranging for the little brother or sister who tends to dominate visitors to be elsewhere for a few hours.

• Role-play friendly and unfriendly behaviours

A simple way to show your child what it takes to be friendly is to have some fun role playing together. Act out disgruntled, quizzical and embarrassed faces or happy, sad or shocked bodies. Role-play the ideas below and assess together which look friendly or unfriendly:

– 'The cat's bum face'

– 'Over the moon'

– 'Cool as a cucumber'

– 'As sour as grapes'

– 'Out of the blue'

– 'Feeling like a million dollars'

– 'A face like a torn sock'

– 'As happy as Larry'

– 'A face like thunder'

– 'The ants' pants'

– 'Shocked beyond belief'

– 'Pleased to see you!'

– 'The cat that licked the cream'

– 'Worried sick'.

Children quickly begin to see how their friendly or unfriendly disposition has the power to turn others on or off them.

• Recipes for successful friendships

Do your children know it is one thing to meet new people, but takes an entirely different set of skills to maintain a friendship? These recipes are invaluable. A good idea may be to create a poster together. This strong visual reminder may provide the supportive edge your child needs to persist with placing friendly behaviours into action.

Recipe for MAKING friends
Introduce yourself.
Smile!
Say your name, and look at them as you speak.
Ask them a question about themselves.
Listen to their answer.
Find an interest you share and talk about it.
Never brag, or act childish.
Be kind by using a gentle voice and thoughtful words.
Make the best impression you can.

Recipe for KEEPING friends
Show you care.
Always share.
Talk, listen and ask questions about them.
Play together.
Allow them to play with others too.
Give positive feedback. Say what it is you like about them.
Think before you speak.
Friendships are not perfect – things will go wrong.
When something goes wrong, always look for a way to fix it.
Friendships change. That's normal!

- Play detective

Ask your child to name a person they think gets along with others really well. As you identify children with the friendliest behaviours you immediately connect your child to the better role models. Ask them to observe how this person gets along with others and the kind of things they say and do. Ask them to discover whether they are good at turn taking, and why they get along with others so well. Emphasise the idea that this person shows friendly behaviours; the sort of qualities that others like.

- Investigate heroes

A good place to start is to get on line and Google! What you are likely to find is that their hero's celebrated life is actually the result of hard work and dealing with setbacks along the way. Success often has more to do with persistence and the ability to get along with others. Examine the problems they faced and how they got around them. Never underestimate the motivation children draw from this. After all, if their hero did it, so can they.

- Investigate community clubs, groups and associations

Despite everyone's best intentions, school is not always the easiest place for all children to find friendship. For quite a few the best source of social connection takes place outside school where they are able to capitalise on a natural interest they can share with others. There are a myriad of clubs, groups, associations and societies within the local community worth exploring. Ideal situations are usually semi organised by adults. They foster friendship, develop interests and provide opportunities for children and adolescents to exercise their social and emotional muscle. The best place to start is at your local council. They are usually very helpful with this sort of information. Alternatively, ask friends, search the telephone directory or try a web search.

• Practice makes perfect

When it comes to showing friendly behaviours, practice really does help to consolidate how it is done! Using some of the ideas below encourage your child to do a friendly act showing friendly behaviours each day.

– Help bring the shopping in.

– Give Mum or Dad a massage.

– Play someone else's game.

– Make someone a snack.

– Offer help for a while.

– Pick some flowers from the garden and give them to someone.

– Say thank you.

– Give a hug.

– Set the table.

– Clear the table.

– Help with the dishes.

– Ask a family member how their day has been, and listen.

– Feed the pet.

– Take out the garbage.

– Make their bed.

– Tidy up their room.

– Get up in the morning without fuss and be ready on time.

– Smile a lot more.

Photocopiable resources now follow, and don't forget the online resources at www.whatsthebuzz.net.au!

After the Buzz . . . Lesson 4

What's the Buzz?

Guess what? Friendly or unfriendly role-play cards

What's the Buzz?

Guess what?   **Friendly or unfriendly role-play card 1**

You are happy to see a friend at school, so with a smile, a friendly voice and hands by your side you say, 'Hi, how are you today?' Ask the group to guess whether you were friendly or unfriendly. How could they tell?

Focus: successfully combining all the skills

What's the Buzz?

Guess what?   **Friendly or unfriendly role-play card 2**

You are really pleased to see a friend. You grab and shake them very hard saying, 'Hi, guess what I did last night? I've got lots to tell you.' Ask the group to guess whether you were friendly or unfriendly. How could they tell?

Focus: grabbing

What's the Buzz?

Guess what?   **Friendly or unfriendly role-play card 3**

You walk up to someone and smile. You say, 'It's great to see you.' But, you fold your arms, use a flat voice and look at the floor. Ask the group to guess whether you were friendly or unfriendly. How could they tell?

Focus: poor body language

What's the Buzz?

Guess what?   **Friendly or unfriendly role-play card 4**

You walk up to someone with a smile. You say, 'Do you want to do the same as yesterday? That was fun!' Use a voice that shows you like them. Keep good eye contact. Ask the group to guess whether you were friendly or unfriendly. How could they tell?

Focus: successfully combining all the skills

What's the Buzz?

Guess what? Friendly or unfriendly role-play cards

continued . . .

What's the Buzz?

Guess what?   **Friendly or unfriendly role-play card 5**

You rush up to someone. You are angry and have your fists clenched next to your chest. You shout, 'That wasn't fair. You cheated and you'll be sorry.' Ask the group to guess whether you were friendly or unfriendly. How could they tell?

Focus: aggressive behaviours

What's the Buzz?

Guess what?   **Friendly or unfriendly role-play card 6**

You are pleased to see a friend. You rush up and hug them as you say, 'Hi, it's great to see you today?' Ask the group to guess whether you were friendly or unfriendly. How could they tell?

Focus: hugging

What's the Buzz?

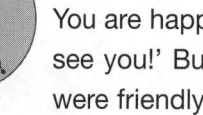

Guess what?   **Friendly or unfriendly role-play card 7**

You walk up to someone. You are not pleased to see them. You do not smile. You do not look at their face. As you say, 'hello' you use a voice that says you don't care about them. Ask the group to guess whether you were friendly or unfriendly. How could they tell?

Focus: deliberately unfriendly

What's the Buzz?

Guess what?   **Friendly or unfriendly role-play card 8**

You are happy to see this person. Using a friendly voice you say, 'Great to see you!' But, you stand too close. Ask the group to guess whether you were friendly or unfriendly. How could they tell?

Focus: proximity

What's the Buzz?

Who's being friendly?

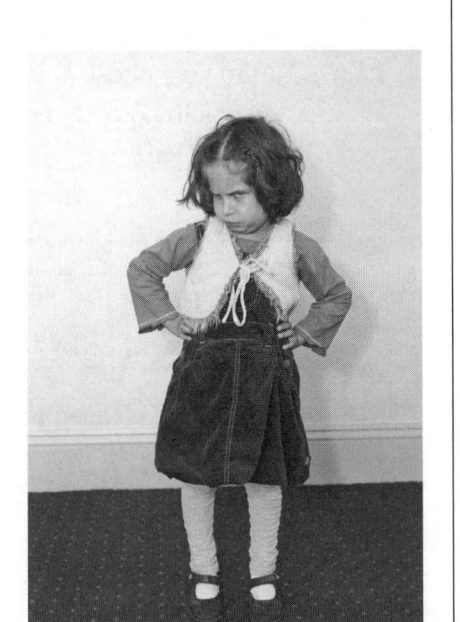

What's the Buzz?

Who's being friendly?

continued . . .

Competition, Winning and Losing

Explanation

All of us like to win. After all, it feels good!' And, the persuasive backdrop to this is the influential media hype that characterises winning as the ultimate goal in competitive sports. Not only do winners bask in the spotlight of accolades, but winning brings fame, wealth, fabulous connections and adoration! On the flip side, competing and having to cope with the disappointment of losing can easily evoke feelings that are difficult, even catastrophic to deal with. Classically, we expect younger children to struggle emotionally with competition and the associated wins and losses.

We often observe that children with delayed social thinking are more seriously challenged by the erratic emotion that accompanies winning and losing. An aspect to appreciate is that these young people have spent a good part of their lives, not only rarely performing as well as their peers, but also being coached, criticised and corrected for making poor social judgements. As a consequence of more failures and setbacks than most, a winning deficit builds. They actually suffer a significant loss: the loss of revelling in the joy of winning. Winning provides every individual the chance to feel capable, skilled and competent in front of peers. Without this sense of winning, frustration and pessimism build, self-esteem suffers and the shadow of resentment over losing is never far away.

This lesson reviews the essential facts about playing games, competition and the inevitability of winning and losing. The students are led to explore practical ideas about what to say and do following a win or a loss. Most importantly, it highlights that the best way to feel like a winner every time is to enjoy the game by playing for fun and friendship. When the goal is fun, winning or losing remains a possibility, but the overriding goal is enjoyment and being well thought of by others.

Materials required for Lesson 5

- Whiteboard/butcher's paper and a marker

- Post *What's the Buzz?* group rules (located on p. 20; alternatively, they can be downloaded from www.whatsthebuzz.net.au)

- Place an outline of the lesson on the whiteboard/butcher's paper

- Prepare the 'Win–lose statement cards' for *Show me the Buzz* (located in the photocopiable resources at the end of this lesson; alternatively, they can be downloaded from www.whatsthebuzz.net.au)

- Four packs of old playing cards for the game 'Tower of Cards'

- One newspaper (or similar) for the game 'Newspaper Race'

- Chairs for the game 'Musical Chairs'

- Four balls of string for the game 'Ball of String Relay'

- A tray, a large, thick towel and six interesting items students can touch for the game 'Can You Guess?'

- Organise the gold nuggets, cubes to build a friendship wall, group rule and reminder cards or a similar feedback device (see the chapter, Practical Considerations)

- Organise a small gift or a reward token for each child

- Prepare handouts for parent(s):

  - One copy of this lesson for each parent to read

  - One copy of *After the Buzz: social thinking ideas for parents* for each parent to read (section follows this lesson).

Lesson 5

Arrange participants into a social circle. Welcome them.

Draw everyone's attention to the group rules. Display the gold nuggets, cubes to build a friendship wall, group rule and reminder cards or a similar motivational device to encourage positive social behaviours (see section on feedback ideas in the chapter, Practical Considerations). As you introduce the idea, and have the attention of students, pick up a gold nugget, a cube, a reminder card or similar to reinforce their cooperative spirit. Explain that if successful each student may leave with a small gift.

1. What's the Buzz?

What's the Buzz? introduces students to this lesson's topic and the new set of skills to be learned. This lesson presents the facts about competition and how to best deal with winning and losing. It also delivers to the group an amazing plan to help them look like and feel like a winner every time, even though they may not win the game itself. The lesson naturally builds on from the previous lesson as students learn being a true winner means encompassing the use of friendly behaviours.

Move through the following swiftly simply to check if participants have these understandings.

FIVE FACTS about playing games, winning and losing

1 When you play games you will win, lose or draw.

2 Winning is exciting. It feels good.

3 Losing is disappointing. It does not feel good.

4 Angry or whining losers look bad and are not liked.

5 Play to have fun during the game – not to just win at the end!

(Write these 'FIVE FACTS' on the whiteboard/butcher's paper)

How to be a TRUE WINNER

'You are a TRUE WINNER when you have fun playing the game. A TRUE WINNER knows that showing friendly behaviours is more important than the winning bit of the game.'

(Write 'How to be a TRUE WINNER' on the whiteboard/butcher's paper)

When you win

1 Enjoy it. It is alright to feel excited.

2 Smile.

3 Shake hands with the person who has lost and say, 'Good game' or 'That was close' or 'I had a lucky break' or 'thanks for that. It was fun.'

4 Do not go on about how you won because it is bragging.

When you lose

1 Keep calm.

2 Think a helpful thought:

   – 'I may be disappointed, but that was fun.'

   – 'It's okay; win some, lose some.'

   – 'This is just a game.'

   – 'Hey, it won't kill me.'

   – 'There will always be another time.'

3 Use a friendly face, body and voice. Say something friendly to the winner:

   – 'Good game.'

   – 'Awesome game.'

   – 'Well done.'

   – 'You deserved to win this time.'

   – 'You played really well.'

   – 'Do you want to play again?'

   – 'You were very good.'

4 Never show your frustration by shouting, swearing, crying, hitting, running away or accusing the winner (or an umpire) of cheating.

5 After the loss, you might want to do something that will cheer you up. Something like stopping at a shop for a drink on the way home can help.

2. Show me the Buzz

Show me the Buzz gives students the opportunity to practise and show they understand the new skill set.

Assist students to form pairs. Spread the 'Statement cards' face down on the floor ready for selection. Ask each pair to choose one 'friendly losing statement card' and one 'friendly winning statement card'. The task is for them to create a short role-play using the statements on the cards selected.

Once pairs have practised ask them to show their role-play to the group. They may need to set the scene to the audience before they show the play. For example, 'This is me on a Saturday morning after my soccer game. We've lost again and I'm walking up to one of the players on the other team . . .'

Statement card: a friendly losing statement

- 'Good game.'

- 'Awesome game.'

- 'You deserved to win.'

- 'You played really well.'

- 'You're so good at this.'

- 'How do you play that well?'

- 'Thanks for the game.'

- 'Do you want to play again?'

Statement card: a friendly winning statement

- 'Good game.'

- 'Thanks for playing.'

- 'That was close.'

- 'Do you want to play again?'

- 'You played really well too.'

- 'I had a lucky break.'

- 'Everything went right this time.'

- 'Thanks for that. It was fun.'

3. Do you know the Buzz?

Move along as quickly as possible to quiz students on the concepts they have learned in the lesson. Encourage everyone to have a go. Let's play!

Round 1

Choose group members to answer each of these questions:

1   Tell me a friendly statement you could say when you win a game.

2   Tell me a friendly statement you could say when you lose a game.

3   Tell me the best plan to be a TRUE WINNER every time.

Round 2

Listen carefully because some of the following statements are true and others will be false. After I have read a statement put your thumbs up if you think it is true. If you think it is false put your thumbs down. If you think it is more complicated than that put your thumbs to the side, but be prepared to tell us what you think!

Statements

1   Most people like to win and that's all right.

2   Winners are skilful and losers are unskilful.

3   It's okay to look disappointed when you lose.

4   When you play a game you will win, lose or draw.

5   When you lose and act badly you will look silly to others.

6   When you play for fun you will always have friends.

7   When you 'brag' about winning others will get annoyed or bored.

8   It's all right to cheat as long as no one catches you.

9   A friendly face, a friendly body and friendly words are always best.

10   Showing disappointment over losing is wrong.

11   Using words such as 'I hate this game' or 'You cheated' is bad.

12   When you play to have fun – not just to win – you give yourself the best chance of making friends.

4. The Buzz

During *The Buzz* students play games that help strengthen the skills central to the lesson. The more group members are encouraged to play these, and similar games, the more opportunity they have to generalise their social thinking and social skills into their day-to-day interactions. As you arrange these games remind students about the friendly things they can do as they play:

1   Let someone else go first.

2   Encourage others: 'good luck', 'great shot', 'wow', 'unreal', 'unbelievable', 'too cool.'

3   Be patient, enjoy watching the others and smile!

4   Give compliments such as: 'you did really well', 'you're good at that', 'you've got talent!'

5   When you lose try not to show your disappointment. Instead, think a helpful thought and show your happiness for the winner.

Individual games

Tower of Cards (passive for older students)

If possible use old playing cards as new cards are quite slippery. Provide each student with half a deck of playing cards. Explain that the aim is to build a tower as high as possible. Discuss and experiment with different designs. Give students a five-minute time limit. Choose a winner and place getters.

Newspaper Race (exciting for all ages)

Each player requires two sheets of newspaper. On 'go' each child races across the room to a wall or a designated turning point. Once they reach it the only way back is to use their sheets of newspaper to step on. Each player will have to lay a sheet of newspaper on the ground, step on it, and then lay the next one down ready to move across to it as they pick up the previous one ready to be used again. The game finishes when all players have returned to the starting point. Naturally, the first player back wins! This is a highly competitive game and takes on a different complexion if you insist that to win the newspapers cannot be torn.

Musical Chairs (exciting for all ages)

For this highly competitive game place half of the chairs side by side, and then arrange the other half with their backs touching the first lot of chairs. Start with each group member sitting on a chair. When the music starts the students stand and begin to walk around the chairs in a clockwise direction. At this moment quickly remove one of the chairs. When the music stops each student must immediately sit down on a free chair, and the player who misses out on a chair is out of the game. Take away another chair and repeat until there are two players and one chair left. You may, at this point, have to create quite a long circuit for the two remaining players to walk around. Of course, the one to sit down first when the music stops wins!

Team games

Animal Relay (exciting for younger students)

Help the children form two lines with equal numbers in each team. Give each player the name of an animal. To illustrate this, all first players might be 'kangaroos'. When told to 'go' the kangaroos must hold their paws up and jump with feet together just as kangaroos do. They are also expected to make continuous sounds similar to that animal. Players travel to an agreed spot and return to tag the waiting player.

Lesson 5

The waiting player moves off using the movement and sound specific to their animal and the first player moves to the back of the line. Good fun animals include rabbits, dogs, cats, crocodiles, eagles, bears, gorillas, jumping fleas, mosquitoes, cockroaches, etc.

Ball of String Relay (exciting for older students)

Arrange the players into two teams. Each team stands in a line (even if there are just two players per team). The captain holds tightly on to the end of the string and the next in line holds the ball of string. On 'go,' the player holding the ball of string runs to a chair on the other side of the room and winds the string twice around the back of the chair, and runs back to the captain. The ball of string is passed to the next player and they run with it winding it twice around the chair and returning to the team. When no players are left to run the captain drops the end of the string they have been holding, takes the ball of string and retraces the steps of previous players winding the string back onto the ball. The first captain back with all the string rewound into a ball wins!

Can You Guess? (exciting for all ages)

Arrange the players into two teams and sit them opposite one another. Help each team to choose a team captain. The captain will need a sheet of paper and a marker to record information for their group. Ask all players to close their eyes for a few moments. While they do this, place six small items on a tray. Place it on the floor between the two teams and cover it with a thick, large towel. Tell players that there are six items on the tray. Select a person from team one to slide a hand gently under the towel and feel the objects. Ask them to tell the captain what some of them might be. Remind them to whisper. Next, select a player from team two to do the same. Move from person to person, team to team, until the captains are satisfied they have all items recorded. The team who guesses correctly wins!

5. Goodbye Buzz

Bid students a warm goodbye and remind them to take their folders, which contain:

- a copy of this lesson for parents

- a copy of *After the Buzz: social thinking ideas for parents.*

As feedback for thoughtful behaviours each student may leave with a small gift.

After the Buzz: social thinking ideas for parents

Lesson 5: Competition, Winning and Losing

This lesson reviewed the facts about competition, winning and losing. It promoted the idea that the best way to feel like a winner every time is to enjoy the game by playing for fun and friendship. The lesson also explored practical ideas about what to say and do following a win or loss. Here are a few sensible ideas parents can use at home to support their children's capacity to cope with winning and losing.

• Highlight what you value

Show that you value the process of playing every game in a friendly way. Winning may well be a goal, but should not be seen as the single most important product of playing games. Discuss aspects such as: laughing, enjoyment, companionship, sharing, intimacy, learning, helping, supporting, teaching, modelling, caring, practice, giving it a go, personal best and so on. With this in mind you might like to play several of the games played in the lesson at home.

• Grow through losing

Although we live in times where it is fashionable to have all children feeling as though they are winners rather than being exposed to the disappointment of losing, one can't help wincing about the short-sightedness of this contemporary thinking. Perhaps, in measured amounts, it can be helpful because through experiencing losing our children learn:

– none of us are good at all things and nor are we expected to be

– we lose because we were not as skilled as the other person at that time

– to appreciate the winner's talent in the context of humanity's astounding diversity

– effort and commitment can never be taken away

– how to re-group their emotions, bounce back, persist and strive

– how good it feels to honestly win or succeed

– to control feelings by being gracious in the face of defeat or disappointment.

• Winning – maybe or maybe not

Prior to your child participating in any kind of game raise the fact that they have a chance of winning and losing. That's the way it is! Remind them to do their best, enjoy and play for personal satisfaction. Continue to encourage them to promote themselves in the best light as this will persuade others to think well of them.

- Home practice

  By rehearsing what your child can do when things don't work out you give them the chance to pre-think or intellectualise a tricky situation. Later, as they draw on their coping skills this earlier work provides them with a helpful edge. A supportive idea is to play games with your child at home. Allow them to win, but discuss how you are enjoying the game and their company first and foremost. When you lose demonstrate friendliness and graciousness. However, from time to time, aim to win the game and coach your child to react well. As they lose jump in and say, 'Great game. I could see that you were disappointed.' 'You're a good sport. I'm impressed!'

- Watch winners and losers

  Whether your child's team wins or loses, point out the players who handle the situation best. Ask, 'How did they act?' 'What did they do?' Also, watch how the players in televised sporting matches handle their emotions after winning or losing. Generally speaking, players at the top level model impeccable skills and this is worth drawing your child's attention to. And, on the odd occasion where a player does something inappropriate, then you have just scored a golden teachable moment!

- Competitive sports

  Parents often ask about the value of their child joining a sporting club as a means to improve friendship and attitudes around competition. In our experience this is questionable. For children who do not have well developed social or sporting abilities, and find losing just too much to bear, the pressure cooker atmosphere of competition can be devastating. It's not long before their frequent emotional meltdowns build a reputation they could well do without.

- What should I do when my child tantrums in public after losing a game?

  There are a few guiding principles worth keeping in mind. When your child becomes thoroughly overwhelmed it is not the time to give advice, lecture or tell them off. A sensible approach is to calmly and swiftly remove them from the situation. What they need is time to regroup their emotions without looking ferocious or silly to others. Sometimes it is wise to invite another level-headed adult, such as the coach, to carefully intervene. Later, in calmer times, discuss what happened and how it can be better handled next time. Sometimes the best decision is to suspend their participation in highly competitive sports for twelve months, which may offer them time to mature.

Photocopiable resources now follow, and don't forget the online resources at www.whatsthebuzz.net.au!

After the Buzz . . . Lesson 5

What's the Buzz?

Win–lose statement cards

STATEMENT CARD

What's the Buzz?

role-play 1

a friendly <u>losing</u> statement

'Good game'

Focus: showing friendly behaviours after losing

STATEMENT CARD

What's the Buzz?

role-play 2

a friendly <u>losing</u> statement

'Awesome game'

Focus: showing friendly behaviours after losing

STATEMENT CARD

What's the Buzz?

role-play 3

a friendly <u>losing</u> statement

'You deserved to win'

Focus: showing friendly behaviours after losing

STATEMENT CARD

What's the Buzz?

role-play 4

a friendly <u>losing</u> statement

'You played really well'

Focus: showing friendly behaviours after losing

What's the Buzz?

Win–lose statement cards

continued . . .

What's the Buzz?

STATEMENT CARD

role-play 5

a friendly <u>losing</u> statement

'You're so good at this'

Focus: showing friendly behaviours after losing

What's the Buzz?

STATEMENT CARD

role-play 6

a friendly <u>losing</u> statement

'How do you play that well?'

Focus: showing friendly behaviours after losing

What's the Buzz?

STATEMENT CARD

role-play 7

a friendly <u>losing</u> statement

'Thanks for the game'

Focus: showing friendly behaviours after losing

What's the Buzz?

STATEMENT CARD

role-play 8

a friendly <u>losing</u> statement

'Do you want to play again?'

Focus: showing friendly behaviours after losing

What's the Buzz?

Win–lose statement cards

continued . . .

STATEMENT CARD

What's the Buzz?

role-play 1

a friendly <u>winning</u> statement

'Good game'

Focus: showing friendly behaviours after winning

STATEMENT CARD

What's the Buzz?

role-play 2

a friendly <u>winning</u> statement

'Thanks for playing'

Focus: showing friendly behaviours after winning

STATEMENT CARD

What's the Buzz?

role-play 3

a friendly <u>winning</u> statement

'That was close'

Focus: showing friendly behaviours after winning

STATEMENT CARD

What's the Buzz?

role-play 4

a friendly <u>winning</u> statement

'Do you want to play again?'

Focus: showing friendly behaviours after winning

What's the Buzz?

Win–lose statement cards

continued . . .

What's the Buzz?

STATEMENT CARD

role-play 5

a friendly <u>winning</u> statement

'You played really well too'

Focus: showing friendly behaviours after winning

What's the Buzz?

STATEMENT CARD

role-play 6

a friendly <u>winning</u> statement

'I had a lucky break'

Focus: showing friendly behaviours after winning

What's the Buzz?

STATEMENT CARD

role-play 7

a friendly <u>winning</u> statement

'Everything went right this time'

Focus: showing friendly behaviours after winning

What's the Buzz?

STATEMENT CARD

role-play 8

a friendly <u>winning</u> statement

'Thanks for that. It was fun'

Focus: showing friendly behaviours after winning

Identifying Feelings

Explanation

Each of us experience feelings. They are a natural emotional response to events that come our way. Sometimes they are wonderful and make us happy, proud, satisfied or excited. At other times they are frightening, hurtful or disappointing, and have the propensity to fuel angry retaliation or intense withdrawal.

One of the most challenging things about being a child is that physical, psychological and neurological development is far from complete. That's right, children are young and clumsy and still gathering experiences. They are bound to make poor judgements and mistakes in response to their feelings. It's what young, inexperienced learners do! A healthy starting point is to appreciate that each one of our children is in absolute rehearsal when it comes to identifying their feelings, processing them and dealing with them constructively. Maturation has not yet offered them the same set of sophisticated social, emotional and communicative abilities we have as adults. To make matters worse, their 'impulse control'— that lifesaving ability to stop and think through situations before they act — is still developing. Yet, life delivers a rich array of experiences to children and each one has the potential to trigger an abundance of emotions.

As parents and teachers, we can support the social thinking of youngsters by teaching them how to:

- understand what causes feelings

- predict situations likely to trigger particular feelings

- identify feelings

- find constructive ways to deal with them.

With this guidance, children can continue to learn, adapt and grow as they meet new challenges.

This lesson is the first of four with an emphasis on feelings. It aims to help students identify their own feelings and the feelings of others. In addition, it teaches children to pre-empt or predict situations that are likely to cause a rush of any particular feelings.

Materials required for Lesson 6

- Whiteboard/butcher's paper and a marker

- Post *What's the Buzz?* group rules (located on p. 20; alternatively, they can be downloaded from www.whatsthebuzz.net.au)

- Place an outline of the lesson on the whiteboard/butcher's paper

- Photocopy the eight 'Feelings faces' (located in the photocopiable resources at the end of this lesson; alternatively, they can be downloaded from www.whatsthebuzz.net.au)

- Provide each student with a copy of the 'Different faces, different feelings booklet' for *Show me the Buzz* (located in the photocopiable resources at the end of this lesson; alternatively, they can be downloaded from www.whatsthebuzz.net.au)

- Sets of coloured markers or pens for students to share

- Two small sheets of paper for each student for the games 'What's On a Face?' and 'Guess my feeling?'

- Organise the gold nuggets, cubes to build a friendship wall, group rule and reminder cards or a similar feedback device (see the chapter, Practical Considerations)

- Organise a small gift or a reward token for each child

- Prepare handouts for parent(s):

  - One copy of this lesson for each parent to read

  - One copy of *After the Buzz: social thinking ideas for parents* for each parent to read (section follows this lesson).

Lesson 6

Arrange participants into a social circle. Welcome them. Draw everyone's attention to the group rules. Display the feedback device to encourage positive social behaviours (see section on feedback ideas in the chapter, Practical Considerations). Explain that if successful each student may leave with a small gift.

1. What's the Buzz?

What's the Buzz? introduces students to this lesson's topic and the new set of skills to be learned. Begin by showing the students the eight pictures of 'Feelings faces'. Each face displays a different emotion; happy, sad, angry, surprised, embarrassed, bored, disappointed and shy. Ask participants to name the feeling that each face suggests. Record their suggestions on the whiteboard/butcher's paper. Encourage the expansion of as many feeling states as possible. Finish by asking, 'How many feelings can people experience?' 'Do we experience just one feeling at a time?'

2. Show me the Buzz

Show me the Buzz gives group members an opportunity to practise and show they can interpret the feelings of others based on their appearance.

Provide each student with a copy of the 'Different faces, different feelings' booklet and a marker. Ask students to circle a word in the column that best describes the feeling this person is experiencing. As students work ask why they are making particular judgements. Encourage them to draw arrows from the word they have circled to parts of the faces or body that give vital clues. For example, a furrowed brow may mean someone is worrying, wide open eyes might convey their surprise and clenched fists looks like they are feeling angry!

Booklets may be taken home following the lesson.

3. Do you know the Buzz?

Do you know the Buzz? is a quick quiz format for students. While needing to be fun its purpose is to consolidate the key concepts gathered in the lesson. Encourage everyone to have a go.

Round 1

I will read some statements to you. Some will be true, some will be false and others may be silly. Once I have read the statement put your thumbs up if you think it is true, your thumbs down if you think it's false, and both thumbs to the side if you think the answer is silly! Let's play!

Statements

1 Every person has feelings.

2 People experience one feeling at a time.

3 People experience exactly 135 feelings.

4 Big tough footballers do not have feelings.

5 If you plan for what might happen you will deal with your feelings better.

6 Feeling angry is normal.

7 Most people feel annoyed when the computer freezes!

8 It is best to try to feel happy all the time.

9 I feel hurt when I'm not invited to parties.

10 Try to stay away from people who make you feel bad.

11 Rich people never feel sad or angry because they can buy what they want.

12 Some people can control their feelings better than others.

13 As you learn more about your feelings you will handle them better.

Round 2

Explain that everything we do leads us to experiencing feelings. And, it can get complicated because we can have more than one feeling at a time. For example, you might be excited about your birthday, but very worried about having so many people together who don't know one another. Choose eager participants to tell an imaginative story based on the emotions given in the scenarios below.

Scenarios

1 You have been playing at a friend's all day. When you arrive home you feel angry and jealous. Why? What happened?

2 You and Kym are 'on again' and 'off again' friends. Today at school you felt rejected and embarrassed. Why? What happened?

3 Morgan, Lee and you usually play together at lunch. You absolutely refused to play with them today. You felt disappointed, worried and scared. Why? What happened?

4 It is a special day and you can't stop smiling. You feel happy, excited and lucky. Why? What happened?

5 You and Si are great friends who always have lots of fun. Today, however, you are worried about Si and feel sorry and sad for him. Why? What happened?

4. The Buzz

The Buzz offers students a chance to play lively games to strengthen the ideas being developed. As you would expect the emphasis in *The Buzz* today is for students to practise reading emotions.

What's on a Face? (passive for all ages)

Facial expressions are an important part of communicating. Let's have fun reading them. In this game each player must decide on a feeling (lay the eight 'Feelings faces' used earlier on the floor as a prompt). Ask everyone to choose one of these feelings: happy, sad, angry, surprised, embarrassed, bored, disappointed or shy. Next, each student secretly writes the feeling they have in mind on a small sheet of paper, folds it up and sits on it. Each player takes a turn to show that feeling on their face. It is up to the group to guess. After the group has guessed they are shown the feeling that was written by the player. This is good fun and groups often ask to play several rounds!

Guess My Feeling? (passive for older students)

Write one of these eight feelings on eight individual pieces of paper: happy, sad, angry, worried, surprised, bored, disappointed and shy. Ask players to take one of the pieces of paper from you, read the feeling written on it, fold it up and not tell anyone.

Explain to the group that this is a role-playing game. They are to take it in turns planning a great afternoon to go to the movies together. They will have to organise what to see, where to meet, what time to meet, what to bring, how much money they need and so on. As each person talks about their ideas they must talk and act in a way that mirrors the feeling on their sheet of paper. For example, the person who selected 'worried' might say, 'we have to meet downstairs by the entrance, it's much safer. We don't want anyone getting lost.' The player who chose 'disappointed' may give the impression that they want to come, but feels disappointed by aspects of the planning. The idea is for each player to try and guess what feeling each of the other players was trying to express in the game.

Cowboys and Indians (exciting for all ages)

This game intentionally picks up the tempo. It will get players moving and puffing! Split the group into half (exact numbers are not important). Name one half Indians and the other half Cowboys. Arrange groups so they stand on opposite sides of the room or space; this is home. Next, ask them to turn their backs towards one another. On 'go', teams walk ever so cautiously backwards towards one another. When the players hear you call 'Indians' the Indians chase the cowboys and try to tag them before they reach home. Or, when the players hear you call 'Cowboys' the Cowboys chase the Indians and try to tag them before they reach home. Once tagged, players join the team that tagged them. Continue the game for as long as you like or until one side is completely caught.

5. Goodbye Buzz

Bid students a warm goodbye and remind them to take their folders, which contain:

• a copy of this lesson for parents

• a copy of *After the Buzz: social thinking ideas for parents*

• their completed 'Different faces, different feelings' booklet.

As feedback for thoughtful behaviours each student may leave with a small gift.

After the Buzz: social thinking ideas for parents

Lesson 6: Identifying Feelings

In this lesson your child learned how to recognise their own feelings and the feelings of others with a view to dealing with them more constructively. Here is a compilation of ideas to practise these skills with your child at home.

- Our children learn from us

    The best way to show our children how to handle their feelings is by handling our own as well as we can. When we lose our temper, storm about in frustration or say hurtful comments they watch and learn to do the same. Also be fair to yourself and accept that mistakes are unavoidable, and when they occur, let your child know that you handled a situation poorly. Allow them to learn from your mistakes as well as from the finer moments you offer them.

- Connect the feeling to the situation

    A surprising number of children benefit from direct guidance. So, when your child faces a problem always begin by asking, 'How are you feeling?' The first step is for them to identify what feelings they have by naming them. Next ask, 'What happened to make you feel like this?' This may lead to, 'I feel sad because Eli and Dav wouldn't play with me'. Subsequently you may ask, 'What do you think they were feeling at the time?' This approach provides the best chance to effectively solve problems.

    Be conscious of using a style of language that links feelings to the challenging situation your child faces:

    - *'You sound frustrated. It's annoying when the computer plays up!'*

    - *'You look sad. I know it hurts not being invited to her party. Come on let's do something to cheer you up.'*

    - *'You look pleased with your spelling test results. It was worth studying.'*

    - *'You sound really worried about it. It's okay, it's normal to feel stressed over things like this!'*

    - *'I know you're bothered by it. Come on, I'll help you finish it off. Then you can watch some television.'*

    - *'You have every right to feel angry. That was unfair on you.'*

After the Buzz . . . Lesson 6

- Be a feelings detective

  From the earliest of ages help your child to attach feelings to words. Work at expanding their feelings vocabulary. In conversation use the words that describe feelings; happy, pleased, satisfied, content, sad, angry, excited, embarrassed, huffy, nervy, anxious, shy, jealous, hateful and so on. Discuss the way people in storybooks, magazine pictures, movies and television 'sitcoms' appear and what they are most likely feeling. Discuss facial expressions, voice tone and body language. Help your child to 'socially read between the lines' by getting them to hypothesise about what might have caused those feelings. Guide them to suggest options they might use to deal with them.

- Make a feelings collage with your child

  Search through a few magazines, select and cut out a collection of images showing different emotions on the faces and bodies of people. Fasten them to a large poster sheet, and next to each image write the emotion, and something that may have triggered it. You may wish to scribe for your child as the aim of the activity is healthy discussions around identifying feelings and what triggers them.

- Calm down, talk later

  When your child becomes upset by runaway feelings aim to be a steady, positive influence. To help them calm down, develop a technique they can use to calm themselves. When their feelings are out of control and it's too difficult for them to think rationally, make it a rule not to participate. Teach them that their initial waves of emotion will pass and once they have them in check it is time to talk and problem solve. Sometimes it is helpful to provide children with a journal where they can write or draw their feelings. This simple approach helps them to crystallise thoughts and emotions.

- Sensitive feelings are beautiful

  Encourage children to express their emotions. Guide your child to understand that all of us have feelings and some of us experience them more often and more deeply. Highlight that having deeply sensitive feelings is not a failing. The only problem is choosing unhelpful ways to manage and express them. Discuss whether they are 'a sponge kid' or a 'Teflon coated kid'. Sponge kids seem to absorb every upset or thoughtless comment that comes their way, while the Teflon coated kids have a tough protection that allows unkind and thoughtless comments to slip by. Teaching children to be careful not to wear their heart on their sleeve is another useful expression to use and is a springboard into strategies to help keep sensitive feelings safe.

Photocopiable resources now follow, and don't forget the online resources at www.whatsthebuzz.net.au!

What's the Buzz?

Feelings faces

What's the Buzz?

Different faces, different feelings booklet

What's the Buzz?

Different faces, different feelings booklet *continued . . .*

Place a circle around the feeling word this face suggests to you.

Why do you think this? _____

_____

_____

_____

_____

Draw an arrow from the feeling word to the part of the face or body that gives you a clue.

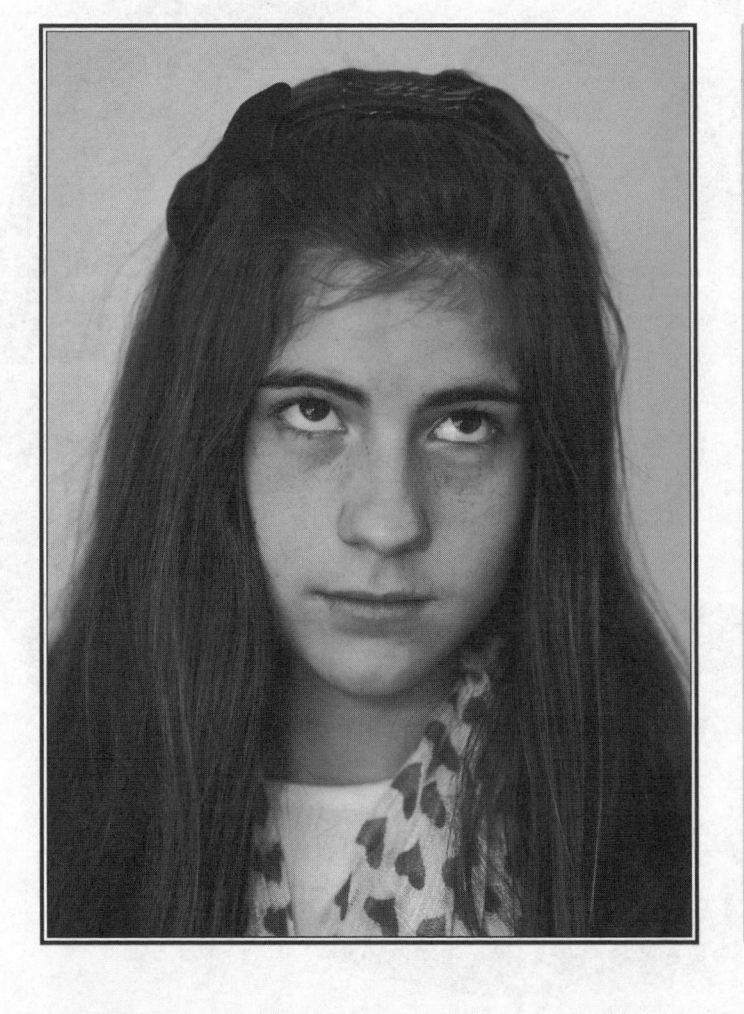

Happy

Sad

Angry

Annoyed

Embarrassed

Bored

Disappointed

Shy

Worried

Sneaky

What's the Buzz? Different faces, different feelings booklet.
Clue: erodb

What's the Buzz?

Different faces, different feelings booklet *continued . . .*

Place a circle around the feeling word this face suggests to you.

Why do you think this? _____

_____

_____

_____

Draw an arrow from the feeling word to the part of the face or body that gives you a clue.

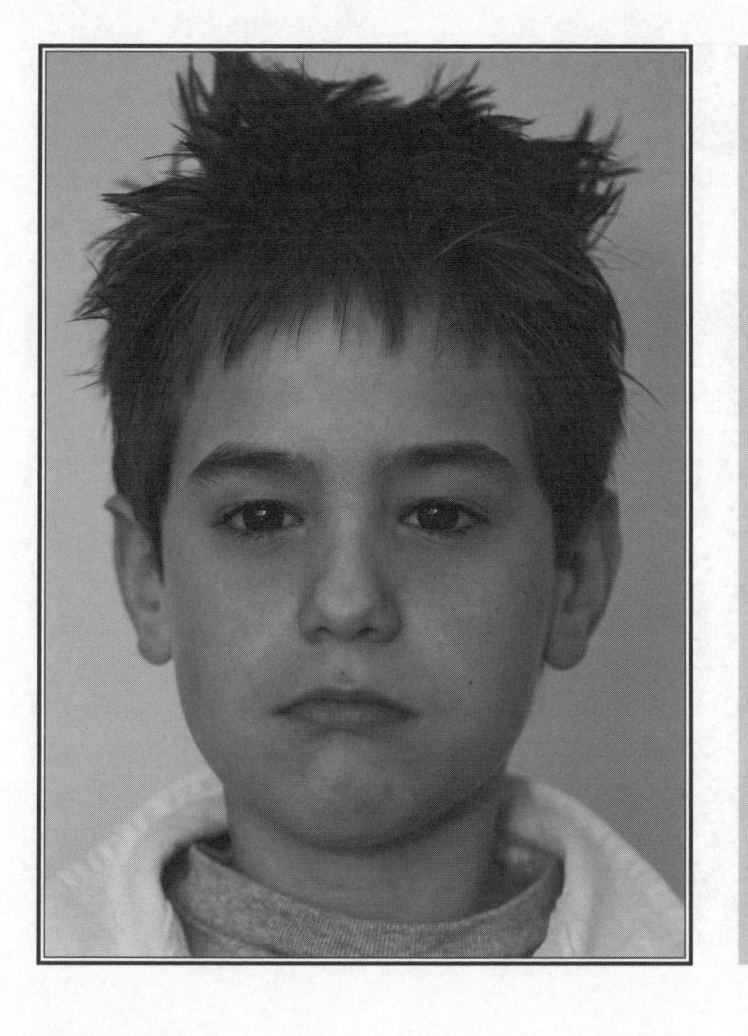

Happy

Sad

Angry

Annoyed

Embarrassed

Bored

Disappointed

Shy

Worried

Sneaky

What's the Buzz? Different faces, different feelings booklet.
Clue: oispinteaddp

What's the Buzz?

Different faces, different feelings booklet continued . . .

Place a circle around the feeling word this face suggests to you.

Why do you think this? _____

_____

_____

_____

Draw an arrow from the feeling word to the part of the face or body that gives you a clue.

Happy

Sad

Angry

Annoyed

Embarrassed

Bored

Disappointed

Shy

Worried

Sneaky

What's the Buzz? Different faces, different feelings booklet.
Clue: kayens

Different faces, different feelings booklet *continued . . .*

Place a circle around the feeling word this face suggests to you.

Why do you think this? _____

_____

_____

_____

Draw an arrow from the feeling word to the part of the face or body that gives you a clue.

Happy

Sad

Angry

Annoyed

Embarrassed

Bored

Disappointed

Shy

Worried

Sneaky

What's the Buzz? Different faces, different feelings booklet.
Clue: baremedrass

Different faces, different feelings booklet *continued . . .*

Place a circle around the feeling word this face suggests to you.

Why do you think this? _____

_____

_____

_____

Draw an arrow from the feeling word to the part of the face or body that gives you a clue.

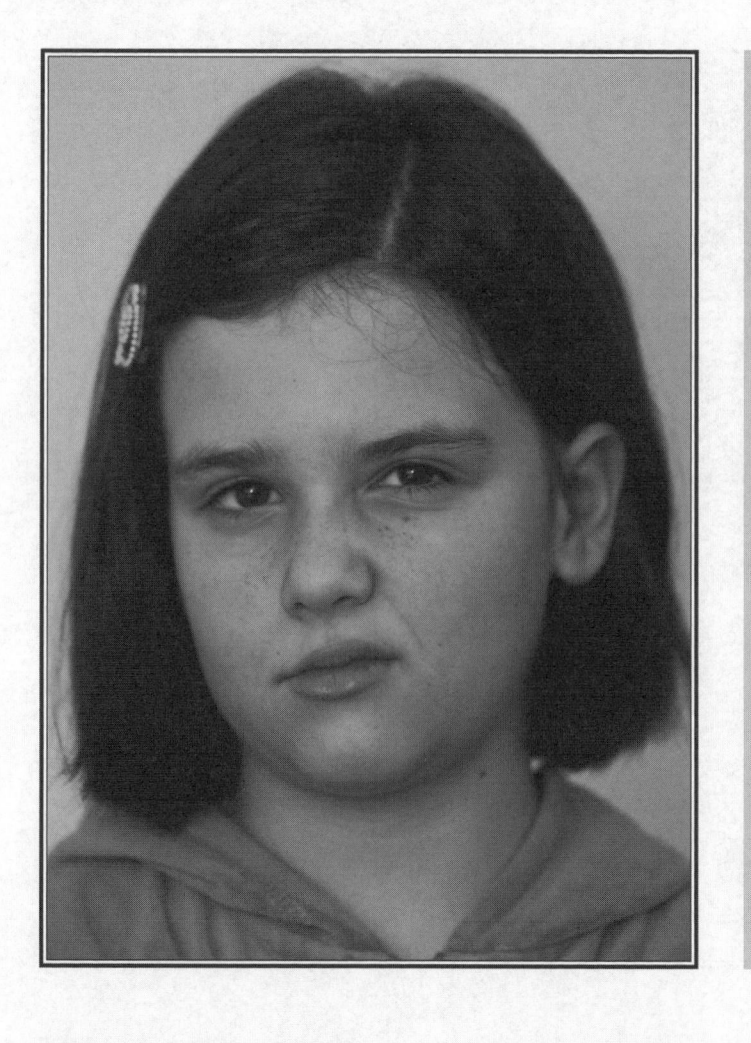

Happy

Sad

Angry

Annoyed

Embarrassed

Bored

Disappointed

Shy

Worried

Sneaky

What's the Buzz? Different faces, different feelings booklet.
Clue: dynnaoe

What's the Buzz?

Different faces, different feelings booklet *continued . . .*

Place a circle around the feeling word this face suggests to you.

Why do you think this? _____

_____

_____

_____

Draw an arrow from the feeling word to the part of the face or body that gives you a clue.

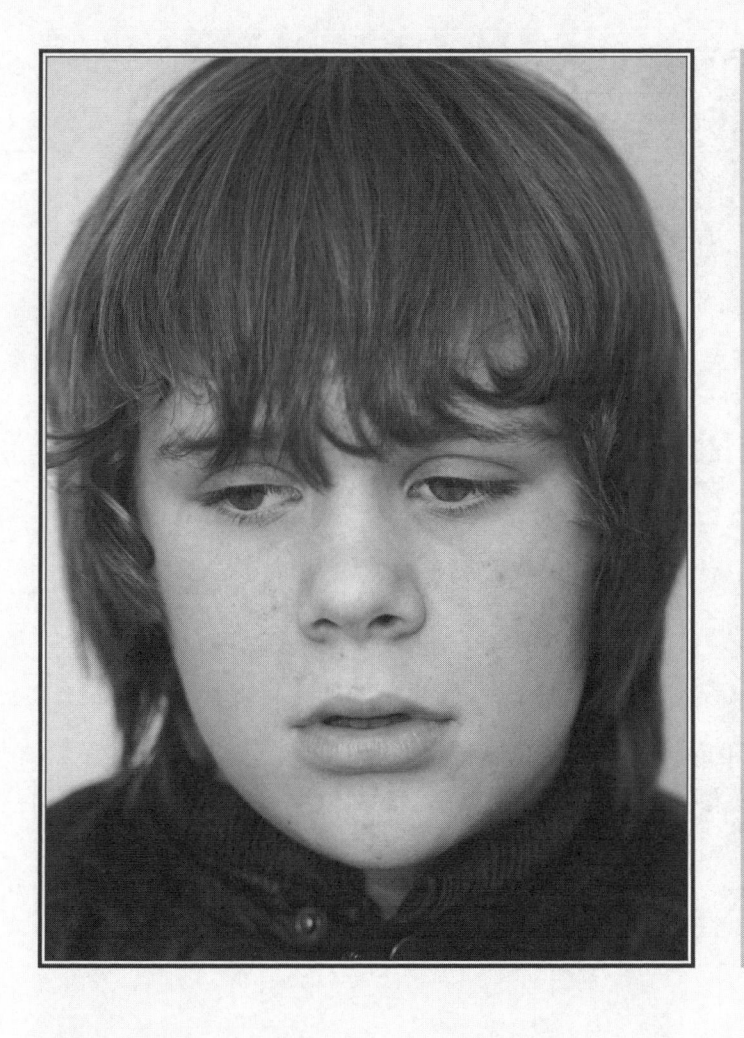

Happy

Sad

Angry

Annoyed

Embarrassed

Bored

Disappointed

Shy

Worried

Sneaky

What's the Buzz? Different faces, different feelings booklet.
Clue: errwiod

Different faces, different feelings booklet *continued . . .*

Place a circle around the feeling word this face suggests to you.

Why do you think this? _____

_____

_____

_____

_____

Draw an arrow from the feeling word to the part of the face or body that gives you a clue.

Happy

Sad

Angry

Annoyed

Embarrassed

Bored

Disappointed

Shy

Worried

Sneaky

What's the Buzz? Different faces, different feelings booklet.
Clue: pahyp

What's the Buzz?

Different faces, different feelings booklet *continued . . .*

Place a circle around the feeling word this face suggests to you.

Why do you think this? _____

_____

_____

_____

Draw an arrow from the feeling word to the part of the face or body that gives you a clue.

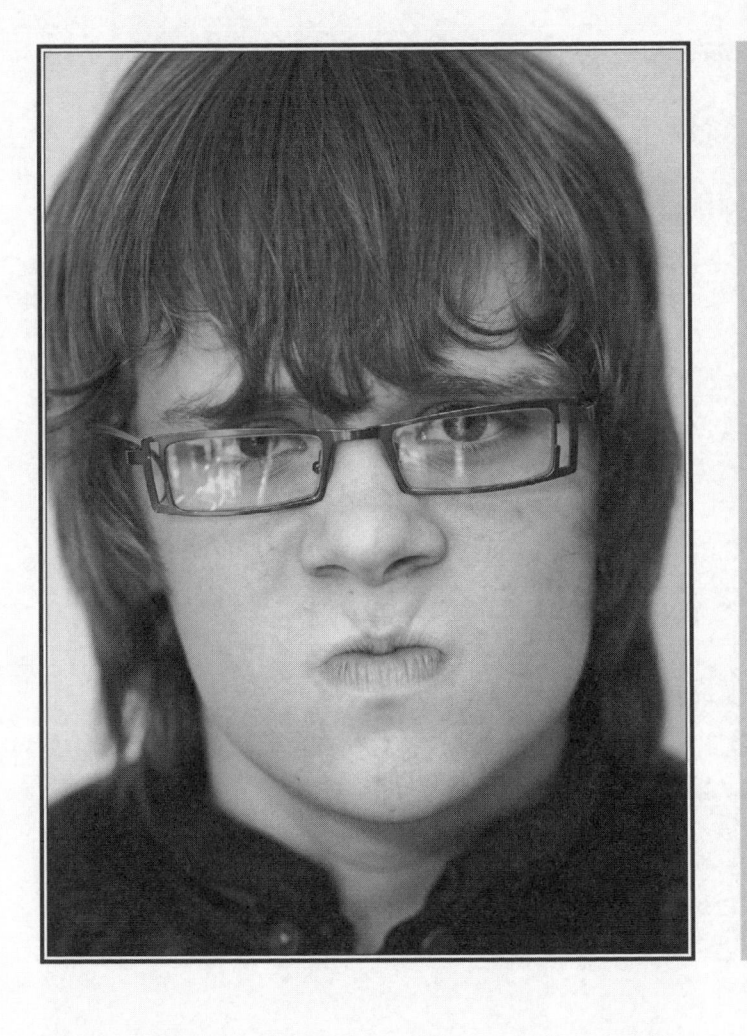

Happy

Sad

Angry

Annoyed

Embarrassed

Bored

Disappointed

Shy

Worried

Sneaky

What's the Buzz? Different faces, different feelings booklet.
Clue: grany

Different faces, different feelings booklet continued . . .

Place a circle around the feeling word this face suggests to you.

Why do you think this? _____

_____

_____

_____

_____

Draw an arrow from the feeling word to the part of the face or body that gives you a clue.

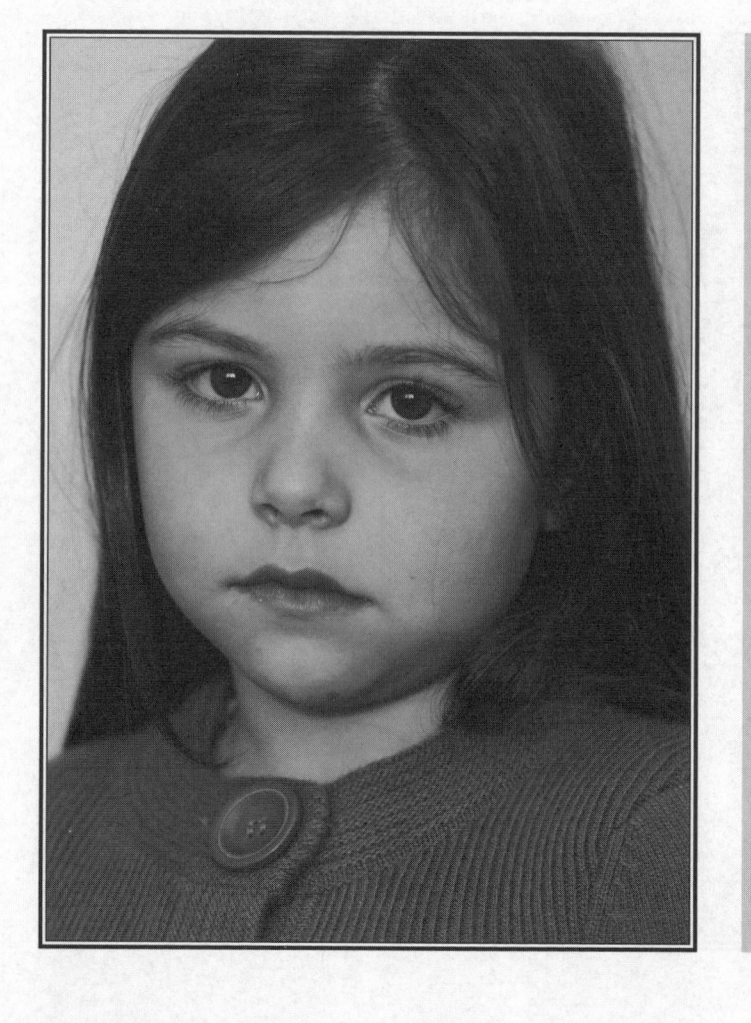

Happy

Sad

Angry

Annoyed

Embarrassed

Bored

Disappointed

Shy

Worried

Sneaky

What's the Buzz? Different faces, different feelings booklet.
Clue: das

Different faces, different feelings booklet *continued . . .*

Place a circle around the feeling word this face suggests to you.

Why do you think this? _____

_____

_____

_____

Draw an arrow from the feeling word to the part of the face or body that gives you a clue.

Happy

Sad

Angry

Annoyed

Embarrassed

Bored

Disappointed

Shy

Worried

Sneaky

What's the Buzz? Different faces, different feelings booklet.
Clue: hsy

Feelings and the Warning Signs

Explanation

This second lesson about feelings takes the focus to 'the warning signs' and how to recognise them.

When our experiences elicit feelings and emotions our bodies transmit physical signals. This is the physical component of our emotions. For example, something that makes us upset is likely to bring on a sensation of tearing up. Similarly, it is common to feel 'a lump in the throat' and 'a racing heart beat' when facing fearful or difficult circumstances. These physical warning indicators alert us to the problems at hand. If we listen to these warnings they can help us to think, and be careful about what we choose to do next. Learning to understand and read these signals prevents taut emotions from being stretched too far and causing us to do things we may regret.

The purpose of this lesson is to teach students to recognise these warning signals.

One of the most powerful benefits arising from the activities is that students are presented with opportunities to talk and listen to others about their own warning signs. This sharing helps to validate feelings that many tend to ignore or misunderstand. As students come to grips with the physiological part of emotion they give themselves the best chance to cope with problematic situations more successfully.

Materials required for Lesson 7

- Whiteboard/butcher's paper and a marker

- Post *What's the Buzz?* group rules (located on p. 20; alternatively, they can be downloaded from www.whatsthebuzz.net.au)

- Place an outline of the lesson on the whiteboard/butcher's paper

- Sets of coloured markers or pens for students to share

- Photocopy two copies of 'Where do your Warning Signs live?' (located in the photocopiable resources at the end of this lesson; alternatively, they can be downloaded from www.whatsthebuzz.net.au)

- Prepare the set of 'Concentration cards' (located in the photocopiable resources at the end of this lesson; alternatively, they can be downloaded from www.whatsthebuzz.net.au)

- One small sheet of paper for each player to play the game 'Moods'

- One small sheet of paper and a roll of tape to play the game 'Who am I?'

- Organise the gold nuggets, cubes to build a friendship wall, group rule and reminder cards or a similar feedback device (see the chapter, Practical Considerations)

- Organise a small gift or a reward token for each child

- Prepare handouts for parent(s):

  - One copy of this lesson for each parent to read
  - One copy of *After the Buzz: social thinking ideas for parents* for each parent to read (section follows this lesson).

Lesson 7

Arrange participants into a social circle. Welcome them. Draw everyone's attention to the group rules. Display the feedback device to encourage positive social behaviours (see section on feedback ideas in the chapter, Practical Considerations). Explain that if successful each student may leave with a small gift.

1. What's the Buzz?

What's the Buzz? introduces students to this lesson's topic and the new set of skills to be learned. Begin by asking:

'Did you know that most feelings give out a warning sign?'

Let me explain; when I feel upset I can get teary. The tears are my warning sign. They are my body's and brain's way of warning me that things are NOT okay, and I need to work out what to do next.

When I'm scared I can get a lump in my throat, find it hard to breathe and my heart beats really fast! This warning sign tells me of the danger I'm facing and that I need to think about what I do next.

Next, ask students to share the sorts of warning signs they feel at different times. Record these on the whiteboard or butcher's paper under two headings:

Warning signs	*Feelings*
teary	upset
lump in throat	scared or worried
cry	afraid or angry
tired or heavy	depressed or sad
headache	stress
sleepy	bored
sweaty hands	nervous or frightened
sweaty all over	really scared
tight arms, chest or throat	fearful
tight body	scared
dry mouth	tense or panicky
heart pounds fast	scared
breathe fast	frightened
run away legs	scared
blush or turn red	embarrassed
funny tummy/'butterflies'	nervous or anxious

Lesson 7

Not surprisingly, students mention very few warning signs connected to feeling happy, contented or proud. Instead, they focus on warning signs associated with feelings of anger, fear and anxiousness. This is the moment to mention the role of adrenalin, the body's natural hormone that places us on high alert. Explain to the group that when our brain believes we are facing a threat our body releases adrenalin. The adrenalin makes our heart beat faster and increases our breathing. This quickly prepares us to either run like the wind to escape the threat, or to stay and protect ourselves. Sometimes the adrenalin just makes us freeze.

2. Show me the Buzz

Show me the Buzz gives students the opportunity to practise and show they understand the new skill set.

Hand each student a worksheet titled, 'Where do your Warning Signs live?' In this exercise direct them to share the coloured markers or pencils. The task is for each participant to connect the warning signs they sometimes experience to a feeling using the blank body.

The idea is for students to build up an inventory of warning signs and feelings while discussing them with other group members. Encourage them to select colours and symbols that match the feeling. To lead students into this activity, show them the example you have creatively completed (located at the end of this chapter).

3. Do you know the Buzz?

Do you know the Buzz? is a quick quiz time for students to consolidate the key concepts gathered to date in the lesson. Encourage everyone to have a go.

Round 1

Arrange the group into a social circle and ask them to listen carefully to the following statements. Some will be true, some will be false and one or two will be silly. After the statement is read students are to put their thumbs up if they think the statement is true, thumbs down if they think it is false, and thumbs to the side if they believe the statement is silly! Let's play!

- Our warning signs usually come at about the same time as the feeling.

- Our warning signs tell us to be careful about what we do next.

- Different people have different warning signs.

- Warning signs are not true.

- When most people get angry their feet tingle. This reminds them to kick.

- Our warning signs are triggered by our feelings.

- A lot of people feel their heart beating fast when they are angry or scared.

- There's no such thing as 'a funny tummy' or 'butterflies in the tummy'. Kids just make it up.

- Weak people have warning signs and brave people do not.

- It is NOT a good idea to ignore a warning sign.

Round 2: CONCENTRATION

1   Cut the CONCENTRATION cards into individual cards (13 matching pairs in total). For younger groups you may wish to use just six or seven pairs.

2   Place them face down on the floor in two parallel rows in the middle of the social circle.

3   Build one row from the cards titled '*What's the Buzz?* CONCENTRATION The feeling'

4   Build the other row from the cards titled '*What's the Buzz?* CONCENTRATION Warning sign'

The group is now ready to play. In this game the cards consolidate the link between 'the feeling' and the 'warning signs' previously discussed. One at a time, players turn a card over from each row hoping to find a match. When a match is made the player keeps the pair of cards and wins a free turn. If the player is not able to match the cards they turn each of the cards face down ready for the next player to try for a match. Keep the game moving quickly. It continues until each pair has been picked up and the player with the most pairs wins!

4. The Buzz

The Buzz offers students a chance to play lively games to strengthen the ideas being developed. Once again the focus today is on several quieter styled games.

Moods (passive for older students)

Hand each player a small sheet of paper or card that has a mood written on it: happy, sad, angry, shocked, exhausted, embarrassed, bored, disappointed and excited. Divide players into pairs. Each person takes it in turn to place their partner's face, body, arms and legs (as if they are a mannequin or dummy) into a position to represent the mood that is on their card. The player who is being manipulated cannot be spoken to and must not know what mood is written on the card. The group must try and guess what the mood is. This is such fun and participants will thoroughly enjoy watching players get moved into various positions!

Who Am I? (passive for all ages)

Arrange the group into the social circle. Tape or clip a piece of paper with a name on it to each player's back (players must not see the name attached to their back). Popular names include: Homer, Marg or Bart Simpson, Spongebob Square Pants, Batman, Superman, Barbie, Ben 10, Dora, Harry Potter, Winnie the Pooh, Cinderella, Santa, Bugs Bunny, Easter Bunny, Scooby Doo, Marvin, Daffy Duck, Tweety, Sylvester, Road Runner and so on. The aim of the game is for each player to find out who they are. Choose a player to start. Ask them to turn their back towards the centre of the circle. At this point all the other players can see the name attached on their back. Next, invite the player to ask questions about who they might be, but the group can only answer with 'yes' or 'no'. Players are successful when they finally ask, 'Am I . . .?' and receive a, 'yes!' It is best to limit this game to two or three turns and follow up in subsequent weeks providing students wish to continue.

At the end of the game ask students how they felt during the game. Did they detect any 'warning signs' of frustration or annoyance because they couldn't easily guess their character?

The Detective and the Thief (passive for all ages)

In this game observational skills are the key to success. First, a volunteer to play the role of detective is required. Direct them to leave the room and move well away until invited to come back in. Once the detective has left the room, select someone who wishes to be the thief. In hushed voices, so the detective can't possibly hear, discuss the physical attributes of the thief. When everyone is ready to commence the game invite the detective to enter the room. As the detective enters call out, 'thank you for arriving so quickly. My new mobile phone has been stolen and we need your super detective skills to find the thief and have it returned!'

The detective is permitted to ask two or three questions (depending on the size of the group) and then guess who the thief must be. They can address their questions to any group member, but will only receive a 'yes' or 'no' reply. The detective needs to phrase each question very thoughtfully. For example:

- *'Is the thief a girl?'*

- *'Does the thief have blonde hair?'*

- *'Is the thief tall?'*

- *'Is the thief wearing new blue and white runners?'*

5. Goodbye Buzz

Bid students a warm goodbye and remind them to take their folders, which contain:

- a copy of this lesson for parents

- a copy of *After the Buzz: social thinking ideas for parents*

- the completed 'Where do your Warning Signs live?' worksheet, plus a spare for a parent to complete.

As feedback for thoughtful behaviours each student may leave with a small gift.

After the Buzz: social thinking ideas for parents

Lesson 7: Feelings and the Warning Signs

In this lesson your child learned that their bodies often transmit physical signals when they experience emotion. For example, many of us talk about feeling 'a lump in the throat,' 'a tight chest' or 'a racing heart' when facing fearful or difficult circumstances. This is in fact the physical component of emotion and alerts us to the problem at hand. It is our brain and body's way of telling us to think carefully about what we do next. Here are a few practical ideas for parents to improve their children's capacity to understand and read their emotions.

• Be patient

The children who participate in *What's the Buzz?* are far more reliant on parents who treat them with respect, who speak quietly when reprimanding, who give them time to respond, and can cleverly sidestep until the heat of the moment subsides. These children, more than most, do their best learning when they are composed. It may not be what you wished for, but their journey to gain self-awareness and self-regulation is at a different pace. It is not a matter of unearthing a miraculous 'cure' through a new therapist or a new programme. What is far more powerful is the thoughtful, consistent approach from parents at home.

In the spirit of gentle, persistent encouragement we offer the following . . .

The North Wind and the Sun

A dispute arose between the North Wind and the Sun, each claiming that he was stronger than the other. At last they agreed to try their powers on a traveller to see which could soonest strip him of his cloak. The North Wind had the first try; and, gathering up all the force for the attack, he came whirling furiously down upon the man, and caught up his cloak as though he would wrest it from him by one single effort: but the harder he blew, the more closely the man wrapped it around himself. Then came the turn of the Sun. At first he beamed gently upon the traveller, who soon unclasped his cloak and walked on with it hanging loosely about his shoulders: then he shone forth in his full strength, and the man, before he had got many steps, was glad to throw his cloak right off and complete his journey more lightly clad.

(Aesop)

- Assist your child to identify their early warning signs

Everything that happens to us is experienced both emotionally and physically whether we are aware of it or not. The physical component, what we refer to as the early warning signs, is often felt first. These are activated as our brain tells our bodies that the experience is likely to be pleasing or otherwise. To illustrate this, as we face a fearful encounter our body releases adrenalin. Abruptly, the heart starts to race and there is a tightening of the muscles preparing the body for a classic fight or flight reaction; increased tension in the muscles, elevated heart rate and a state of fear as the emotional centre of the brain tends to reduce emotional strength. Suddenly we think less clearly!

Alert your child to the simple facts. They need to know what is happening to their body and emotions when stressed and conversations often provide a wonderful way to explore this. Simple things such as saying, 'I understand you're angry Stef. I can see how hot and red your face is. I bet your heart is beating fast as well!' By being empathetic and helping youngsters identify their feelings the heat can be taken out of many an emotionally charged situation. This practical day-to-day approach offers the best chance to consolidate a child's understanding about their feelings.

- The smart advantage

Those who learn to stay calm when things go wrong give themselves the advantage of thinking more clearly and making better choices. It's the smart advantage! When someone says something that's annoying, hurtful or threatening a brain that remains calm and can think of new ways to address the problem – a smile, a shrug, walk away, tell a joke, ignore, run, eye roll, duck for cover, be quiet, agree, say sorry or become invisible and blend into the background – gives the best advantage. A smart idea is to teach children to press the 'delete key' in their mind and shrink those they are having trouble with into little babies with smelly nappies. Also teach that just because someone looks as though they are being mean or thoughtless, it isn't a cue to get even, get back at them or have the last say. All children need to know that when they stay calm they give their brain the best chance to send powerful help messages to deal with the problem. When they do this they exude confidence, poise and graciousness and this will have a positive influence on how others see them.

- Where do your Warning Signs live?

Ask your child to share their completed 'Where do your Warning Signs live?' worksheet. It should be in their folder. Also in the folder is a blank worksheet for you to complete. Fill it out with your child. In this way they can learn more about you and how you interpret your warning signs! Comparing similarities and differences provides useful discussion and new learning.

Photocopiable resources now follow, and don't forget the online resources at www.whatsthebuzz.net.au!

What's the Buzz?

Where do your Warning Signs live?

My Example

Connect the warning signs you experience to a feeling.

To give you an idea one has been completed for you.

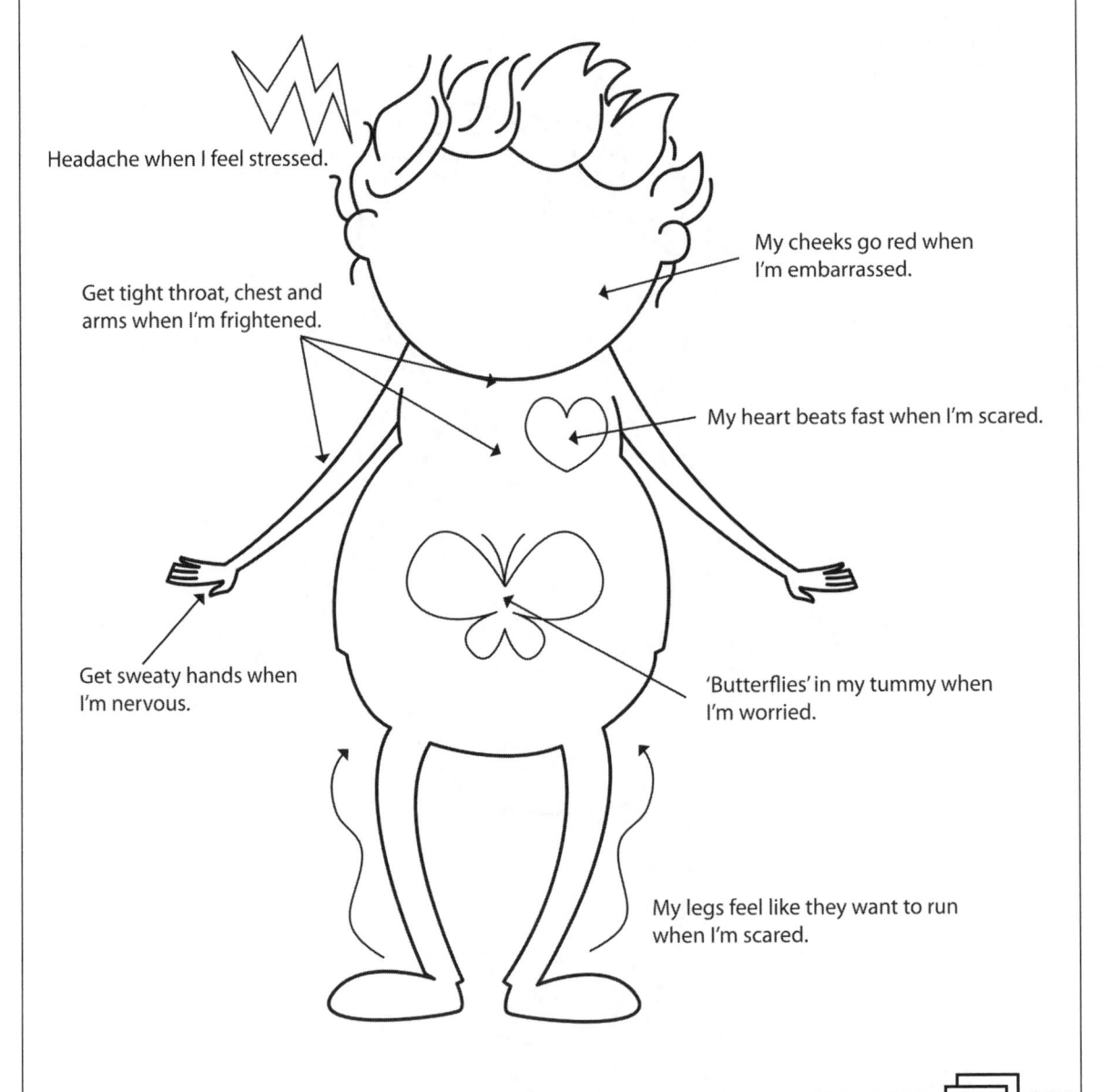

Headache when I feel stressed.

My cheeks go red when I'm embarrassed.

Get tight throat, chest and arms when I'm frightened.

My heart beats fast when I'm scared.

Get sweaty hands when I'm nervous.

'Butterflies' in my tummy when I'm worried.

My legs feel like they want to run when I'm scared.

What's the Buzz?

Where do your Warning Signs live?

Name: _____

Warning Signs	Feelings
teary	upset
lump in throat	scared or worried
cry	afraid or angry
tired or heavy	depressed or sad
headache	stress
sleepy	bored
sweaty hands	nervous or frightened
sweaty all over	really scared
tight arms, chest or throat	fearful
tight body	scared

What's the Buzz?
Concentration cards

What's the Buzz?	CONCENTRATION	The feeling

A Little Upset

What's the Buzz?	CONCENTRATION	Warning sign

Teary

What's the Buzz?	CONCENTRATION	The feeling

Scared or Worried

What's the Buzz?	CONCENTRATION	Warning sign

Lump in Throat

What's the Buzz?	CONCENTRATION	The feeling

Afraid or Angry

What's the Buzz?	CONCENTRATION	Warning sign

Cry

What's the Buzz?	CONCENTRATION	The feeling

Depressed or Sad

What's the Buzz?

Concentration cards *continued . . .*

What's the Buzz?	CONCENTRATION	Warning sign	
Tired or Heavy			

What's the Buzz?	CONCENTRATION	The feeling	
Stressed			

What's the Buzz?	CONCENTRATION	Warning sign	
Headache			

What's the Buzz?	CONCENTRATION	The feeling	
Bored			

What's the Buzz?	CONCENTRATION	Warning sign	
Sleepy			

What's the Buzz?	CONCENTRATION	The feeling	
Nervous or Frightened			

What's the Buzz?	CONCENTRATION	Warning sign	
Sweaty Hands			

What's the Buzz?

Concentration cards *continued . . .*

What's the Buzz?	CONCENTRATION	The feeling
	Very Fearful	

What's the Buzz?	CONCENTRATION	Warning sign
	Tight Arms, Chest or Throat	

What's the Buzz?	CONCENTRATION	The feeling
	Scared	

What's the Buzz?	CONCENTRATION	Warning sign
	Heart Pounds Fast	

What's the Buzz?	CONCENTRATION	The feeling
	Frightened	

What's the Buzz?	CONCENTRATION	Warning sign
	Breathe Fast	

What's the Buzz?	CONCENTRATION	The feeling
	Scared	

What's the Buzz?

Concentration cards *continued . . .*

What's the Buzz?	CONCENTRATION	Warning sign

Runaway Legs

What's the Buzz?	CONCENTRATION	The feeling

Embarrassed

What's the Buzz?	CONCENTRATION	Warning sign

Blush or Turn Red

What's the Buzz?	CONCENTRATION	The feeling

Nervous or Anxious

What's the Buzz?	CONCENTRATION	Warning sign

Funny Tummy/'Butterflies'

Feelings and Thinking Positively

Explanation

As children begin to understand how their feelings can influence the choices they make, it is timely to teach them how to switch to a positive style of social thinking to solve everyday problems. All children should know that when they stay calm they give their brain the best chance to think clearly, to consider others and make the best choices. It is what we call, *'the smart advantage!'*

When faced with a problem a child who thinks positively is more likely to approach it by thinking, 'I won't give up. I'll try this again, but differently'. In contrast, a child who employs negative qualities is more likely to think, 'I'm stupid. I'll never try that again' or 'I hate them now.' 'I'll pay them back tomorrow.' The positive manner in which an individual responds to a setback has long been described as emotional resilience, human durability, emotional toughness or personal flexibility. It is the measure of a person's capacity to cope, to make sense of difficulties and find constructive ways to move forward.

And, why is this so important? According to copious amounts of research, as well as lifelong observations, we know positive thinkers are more inclined to plan, persist, take healthy risks, arrive at better decisions and find greater success in all kinds of ways (Scheier, 1986; Scott, 2002; Seligman, 2002; Seligman, 2006). Positive thinking is a resilient attitude, and it permits each of us to re-examine and regroup our resources and bounce back despite encountering an interruption or problem. Those who make this transition to thinking positively gradually become expert in accessing an assortment of skills essential for lifelong emotional resilience.

This third lesson about feelings takes the focus to making positive choices as a healthy response to the many emotional situations we experience. It highlights the power of thinking positively, and how to do it.

Materials required for Lesson 8

- Whiteboard/butcher's paper and a marker

- Post *What's the Buzz?* group rules (located on p. 20; alternatively, they can be downloaded from www.whatsthebuzz.net.au)

- Place an outline of the lesson on the whiteboard/butcher's paper

- Prepare the set of 'Battle lines' cards (located in the photocopiable resources at the end of this lesson; alternatively, they can be downloaded from www.whatsthebuzz.net.au)

- One small packet of sweets to share during the game 'Battle lines'

- One blindfold and a big armful of books for the game 'Minefield'

- Print Interim Certificates of Achievement (located in the photocopiable resources at the end of this lesson; alternatively, they can be downloaded from www.whatsthebuzz.net.au)

- Organise the gold nuggets, cubes to build a friendship wall, group rule and reminder cards or a similar feedback device (see the chapter, Practical Considerations)

- Organise a small gift or a reward token for each child

- Prepare handouts for parent(s):

  - One copy of this lesson for each parent to read

  - One copy of *After the Buzz: social thinking ideas for parents* for each parent to read (section follows this lesson).

Lesson 8

Arrange participants into a social circle. Welcome them. Announce that at the end of the lesson each participant will receive a *'What's the Buzz?* Interim Certificate of Achievement to mark the half-way point of the programme.

Draw everyone's attention to the group rules. Display the feedback device to encourage positive social behaviours (see section on feedback ideas in the chapter, Practical Considerations). Explain that if successful each student may leave with a small gift.

1. What's the Buzz?

What's the Buzz frames a new set of skills to switch on *positive thinking* and switch off *negative self-talk*. Begin by asking the group:

Do you know how to switch *positive thinking* on?

We create positive thoughts by talking to ourselves confidently. As we do this our bodies relax and our brain believes it can handle the situation. This switches our *positive thinking* on so we are ready to solve problems!

Positive thoughts sound like this (ask students to contribute):

- *'I can handle this.'*
- *'I know I can do this.'*
- *'I'm smart enough to deal with this.'*
- *'I can't control the things people say, but I can control me.'*
- *'I can be confident.'*
- *'I can stay and look calm.'*
- *'I'll just tackle one thing at a time.'*
- *'Everything will be okay, because it usually is in the end.'*

On the other hand, we can also switch negative thinking on.

When we switch on negative thoughts our bodies tense up and our brain thinks that the only way to handle the problem is to fight, run away or freeze.

Negative thoughts sound like this (ask participants to contribute):

- *'It's no use.'*
- *'I'm useless.'*
- *'No one ever believes me.'*
- *'This stuff always happens to me.'*
- *'Who cares I hate them anyway.'*
- *'I'll pay them back tomorrow.'*
- *'I am an idiot.'*

- *'I'm ugly.'*
- *'I'm dumb.'*
- *'There's nothing I can do.'*
- *'I hate them.'*
- *'I'll never go to school again.'*
- *'I'll never try that again.'*
- *'I'm a failure.'*

2. Show me the Buzz

Show me the Buzz offers everyone a chance to practise switching on *positive thinking*. Let's play 'BATTLE LINES' to show how it's done!

The idea is for students to battle a negative thought with a positive thought, because the more we practise this the more emotionally resilient we become.

To begin the facilitator places twelve 'Positive Thought Cards' on the floor in the centre of the social circle. Read them out as they are placed face up on the floor. Stress how valuable this kind of thinking is to deal with life's problems. Next, offer a student the chance to draw one 'Negative Thought Card' from the selection you are holding face down in your hand. Ask them to read the negative thought to the group.

The student's task is to battle this negative thought by matching it with a positive thought card on the floor. To do this they must grab the best positive thought and read it out loud. If the group believes the match is appropriate the student is awarded a small sweet. This is not a winning and losing game. All players are rewarded for enthusiastic participation and participants are encouraged to help one another.

12 'NEGATIVE thought cards'	12 'POSITIVE thought cards'
(to be held face down in the facilitator's hand)	*(to be read out as placed face up on the floor)*
'This will be too hard for me. I'll never do it.'	'I can do it. I'm as good as anyone.'
'He's such a show off. I hate him.'	'Maybe he shows off because he needs friends.'
'I'm not doing this. She can't make me.'	'I'll give it a try. I'll see how it goes.'
'Mum won't believe me so I won't tell her.'	'I could say, "Sorry Mum" and tell her the truth.'
'I feel bad today. I deserve to be lonely.'	'I'll try to join in. It will probably make me happier.'
'Who cares? It's not worth it anyway.'	'I should give it a go. It might be worthwhile.'
'Mum and Dad never let me have friends over.'	'I'll ask if Sam could come over when we get back.'
'I'm so angry. I'll show them. I'll smash their stuff.'	'I need to think. Anger won't help me.'
'I hate homework. I don't feel like doing it.'	'Homework is boring. I'll do it bit by bit.'
'I was not out. I will not go out. Try and make me!'	'Maybe I was out. I should just go with it.'
'She had no right to say that. I'll get her back.'	'I can't control what she said, but I can control me.'
'She's a liar. She's always lying.'	'I bet she lies to impress people.'

3. Do you know the Buzz?

Do you know the Buzz? is a quick quiz format. Its purpose is to consolidate the concepts gathered so far.

Round 1

Read each of the following scenarios, and the thinking statements, to the group. Their challenge is to decide which ideas are based on *positive thinking*. Ask students to put their thumbs up when they hear positive problem solving and thumbs down when they hear negative thinking or self-talk. Let's play!

Scenario 1

Your computer shuts down. It saves, but cannot be restarted. Your assignment is due tomorrow and it is very important. You will not be able to print out your work until the computer is repaired and this may take two weeks.

Thinking . . .

- *'I've done the assignment. I'll tell my teacher what happened and we'll work it out together.'*

- *'I'm dead. My teacher never believes anything.'*

- *'I'll tell my teacher that mum was sick last night and we had to go to hospital with her.'*

- *'This stuff always happens to me. Why bother trying?'*

- *'Who cares? I hate school anyway.'*

- *'Mum and Dad saw my assignment anyway. They can help me explain what went wrong to the teacher.'*

Scenario 2

An older student at school has threatened you by bumping you into a wall. He makes you feel frightened. So do his friends. This is the third time he's done it this week.

Thinking . . .

- *'I probably deserve this.'*

- *'I usually get bullied because I'm small.'*

- *'I can't control him, but I can control what I do.'*

- *'Nothing ever works.'*

- *'I need to look calm and be calm.'*

- *'I need to think about who can help me.'*

- *'Things always go wrong for me.'*
- *'I'll never go to school again.'*
- *'I need to talk to my teacher again.'*
- *'I'll get a gang of kids together and get him after school.'*

4. The Buzz

The Buzz offers students the opportunity to play lively games to strengthen the newly acquired ideas. Today three games are planned.

Find the Leader? (passive for all ages)

Sit everyone in a social circle. Select one person as an official detective and ask them to leave the room for a few moments. While the detective is away choose one person to lead the group.

As the detective returns to the room the leader may, for example, have everyone clapping in rhythm. Then, after about thirty seconds the leader changes their action to finger waving. And so, the leader continues to change their action every so often and the group must quickly follow. New actions might include: raising and lowering eyebrows, clapping fingers, winking, poking out tongues, head rolling, pulling at one or both ears, leg slapping, on and off smiling.

The detective's aim is to discover the leader. This requires sharp listening and looking skills on behalf of the leader, the detective and the group. This is such fun!

Minefield (exciting for all ages)

At the heart of this game is *positive talk* and encouraging communication. Let the group watch as you scatter a range of objects (books, shoes, jumpers, etc) over the floor. They are the mines. Next, arrange participants into pairs. Choose a pair to begin while the others watch on. The idea is that one of the pair chooses to be a trusted guide and the other is blindfolded. Once blindfolded, spin the player around several times to disorient them slightly, then the game begins! At this point the guide may not touch their partner, and may only use words to direct his or her partner through the minefield. If the blindfolded player stumbles on to a mine the pair must go back to the start. The idea is to make it to the other side unharmed.

Chinese Whispers (passive for all ages)

This old favourite always draws a laugh. Sit everyone in a large circle so there is plenty of space between the players. Whisper a phrase or a sentence into the ear of a student sitting next to you. Make the phrase more complex for older students. This first student then whispers the phrase ever so quietly to the next, and in turn, the whisper travels from one to another right around the circle. The last person to receive the message announces what they have just heard. Rarely is it the same phrase or sentence that began the journey!

5. Goodbye buzz

Bid students a warm goodbye and remind them to take their folders, which contain:

- a copy of this lesson for parents

- a copy of *After the Buzz: social thinking ideas for parents*

- *What's the Buzz?* Interim Certificates of Achievement. Hand a Certificate of Achievement to students. Tell each student something special you have noticed about their learning and progress.

As feedback for thoughtful behaviours each student may leave with a small gift.

After the Buzz: social thinking ideas for parents

Lesson 8: Feelings and Thinking Positively

The aim of this lesson is to highlight to students the power of thinking positively, and how to do it. Here are some practical approaches parents can use at home to switch their children's emerging positive thought patterns on!

- Sensitive feelings

  Guide your child to see that we all have feelings, but some of us experience them more often and more deeply. Being sensitive is not a weakness. It may in actual fact become your child's greatest asset one day. However, what may be a problem is their inability to find positive ways to express disappointed or hurt feelings, and this of course is where our work lies. Make a clear distinction between the good fortune of having sensitive feelings and the inability to find constructive ways to express them.

- Role model positive thinking

  All children need to know that when they stay calm they give their brain the best chance to think and make the best choices. So, when something goes wrong, try to find the 'silver lining' or a lesson in it. For example, if your car runs out of petrol and you have to walk you might say, 'Running out of petrol is annoying, but it gives me a chance to walk and talk with you.' Similarly, show how to draw on humour when things go wrong. As Monty Python once said, 'always look on the bright side of life!'

- Teach positive self-talk

  Most of us use positive self-talk when we find ourselves thinking through or tackling tricky situations. We might say to ourselves, 'I'll find a way to work this out.' Let your children catch you modelling it because positive self-talk is a reliable way to stay in control, think, persist and find a solution. As mentioned earlier, studies reveal that positive self-talk training helps us find success.

- Teach how to 'switch' to positive thinking

  Every so often show your child how to switch their thinking. When they say, 'I hate cleaning my room' you might say, 'Yeah, it's not fun, but you always feel good once it's done!' Or, when you are confronted by your child complaining about a nemesis at school you might respond with, 'I agree, Jarrod is tough to get along with, but remember he deals with a lot of tough stuff at home.' Do what you can to guide your child to see other perspectives.

- Develop a positive saying of the week

It is surprising how some children will seize on an optimistic saying and use it as an aid. The best sources for these are inexpensive, inspiring little books often found at the local news agency; or use the internet. They are both wonderful resources for these:

- Attitudes are contagious. Are yours worth catching? (Dennis and Wendy Mannering).

- Wherever you go, no matter what the weather, always bring your own sunshine (Anthony J. D'Angelo).

- I had the blues because I had no shoes until upon the street, I met a man who had no feet (Ancient Persian saying).

- Attitude is a little thing that makes a big difference (Winston Churchill).

- Every day may not be good, but there's something good in every day (Author Unknown).

- Happiness is an attitude. We either make ourselves miserable, or happy and strong. The amount of work is the same (Francesca Reigler).

- The only disability in life is a bad attitude (Scott Hamilton).

- If you aren't fired with enthusiasm, you will be fired with enthusiasm (Vince Lombardi).

- I don't like that man. I must get to know him better (Abraham Lincoln).

- Make your optimism come true (author unknown).

- Believe it is possible to solve your problem. Tremendous things happen to the believer. So believe the answer will come. It will (Norman Vincent Peale).

- Feel the difference!

A great way to show your child the difference between thinking positively and negatively is to help them make a set of rose-coloured glasses and set of dark glasses. Use cellophane for the lenses and pipe cleaners for the frames. Next, google a few images, or find images in a magazine of people facing a challenge. Ask your child to put on the rose-coloured glasses and imagine themselves as one of the people in the image thinking in the most positive way. What would they be thinking or saying to cope absolutely best with the challenge? Now take off the rose-coloured glasses and put on the dark glasses. The dark glasses change the world into a more negative place where thoughts are pessimistic and gloomy. What would the people in the image be thinking or saying now about the challenge? This is an effective way for children of all ages to feel the difference. We recall doing this with a group of middle primary students. Dakota was the positive voice and another boy chose to be the negative voice in the activity. I should add that while Dakota is highly impulsive and often shows aggression, he deals with a pretty tough life at home. They both stared intently at the challenging image and offered a variety of ideas. Both generated

After the Buzz . . . Lesson 8

a string of creative suggestions, but Dakota's positive self-talk was on fire! After we'd finished, he came up to me and said, 'You know. . .I did good didn't I? I ought to listen to that stuff myself!'

- Make a 'Positive Ways to Think' chart

Display it on a wall at home as a visual reminder for everyone to think, talk and act in constructive ways. Here are a few positive thought starters . . .

- 'I can handle this.'

- 'I think best when I stay calm and give my brain a chance to think.'

- 'Just one thing at a time.'

- 'This doesn't have to get me down.'

- 'I can talk to someone about it.'

- 'I'm smart enough to get through this.'

- 'It will be okay.'

- 'I can do this.'

- 'I'll have a chat to my cat about it.'

- 'There are a million ways to solve a problem, and I just need to choose one.'

Photocopiable resources now follow, and don't forget the online resources at www.whatsthebuzz.net.au!

After the Buzz . . . Lesson 8

What's the Buzz?
Battle lines

What's the Buzz?	**BATTLE LINES**	**NEGATIVE** Thought Card	
'This will be too hard. I'll never do it.'			

What's the Buzz?	**BATTLE LINES**	**POSITIVE** Thought Card	
'Of course I can do it. I'm as good as anyone.'			

What's the Buzz?	**BATTLE LINES**	**NEGATIVE** Thought Card	
'He's such a show off. I hate him.'			

What's the Buzz?	**BATTLE LINES**	**POSITIVE** Thought Card	
'Maybe he shows off because he needs friends.'			

What's the Buzz?	**BATTLE LINES**	**NEGATIVE** Thought Card	
'I'm not doing this. She can't make me.'			

What's the Buzz?	**BATTLE LINES**	**POSITIVE** Thought Card	
'I'll give this a try. I'll see how it goes.'			

What's the Buzz?	**BATTLE LINES**	**NEGATIVE** Thought Card	
'Mum won't believe me so I won't tell her.'			

What's the Buzz?	**BATTLE LINES**	**POSITIVE** Thought Card	
'I could say, 'Sorry Mum,' and tell the truth.'			

What's the Buzz?

Battle lines *continued . . .*

What's the Buzz?	BATTLE LINES	NEGATIVE Thought Card	
'I feel bad today. I deserve to be lonely.'			

What's the Buzz?	BATTLE LINES	POSITIVE Thought Card	
'I'll try to join in. It'll probably make me happier.'			

What's the Buzz?	BATTLE LINES	NEGATIVE Thought Card	
'Who cares? It's not worth it.'			

What's the Buzz?	BATTLE LINES	POSITIVE Thought Card	
'It might be worthwhile. I should give it a go.'			

What's the Buzz?	BATTLE LINES	NEGATIVE Thought Card	
'Mum and Dad won't let me have Sam over.'			

What's the Buzz?	BATTLE LINES	POSITIVE Thought Card	
'I'll ask if Sam can come over when we get back.'			

What's the Buzz?	BATTLE LINES	NEGATIVE Thought Card	
'I'm so angry. I'll show them. I'll smash their stuff.'			

What's the Buzz?	BATTLE LINES	POSITIVE Thought Card	
'There has to be a better way. Anger won't help!'			

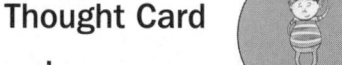

What's the Buzz?

Battle lines *continued . . .*

What's the Buzz?	BATTLE LINES	NEGATIVE Thought Card	
'I hate homework. I won't do it.'			

What's the Buzz?	BATTLE LINES	POSITIVE Thought Card	
'Homework is boring, but I'll try this bit first.'			

What's the Buzz?	BATTLE LINES	NEGATIVE Thought Card	
'I was not out. I won't go out. Try and make me.'			

What's the Buzz?	BATTLE LINES	POSITIVE Thought Card	
'Maybe I was out. I should just go with it.'			

What's the Buzz?	BATTLE LINES	NEGATIVE Thought Card	
'She's a liar. She's always lying.'			

What's the Buzz?	BATTLE LINES	POSITIVE Thought Card	
'I bet she lies to impress people.'			

What's the Buzz?	BATTLE LINES	NEGATIVE Thought Card	
'She had no right to say that. I'll pay her back.'			

What's the Buzz?	BATTLE LINES	POSITIVE Thought Card	
'I can't control what she said, but I can control me.'			

CERTIFICATE OF ACHIEVEMENT

This is to certify that

has successfully completed the first half of *What's the Buzz?*

CONGRATULATIONS!

Awarded on ___ / ___ / ___

Feelings and Ideas to Create Well-Being

Explanation

During previous lessons, one of the central ideas promoted was that each of us experience feelings because they are a natural response to what we encounter in life. This is a powerful message because when young individuals experience intense feelings they can easily believe that nothing can help, except to get caught in a classic fight or flight reaction. Yet, as we know, there are a multitude of ways to solve problems and manage feelings differently.

This fourth lesson about feelings explores ways for children to take care of their emotional health. With a collection of 'calm-down' options to draw from students can begin to trial new ways to manage life stresses more effectively. As they learn how to better manage their well-being the risk of storing frustrations, and suddenly exploding, is minimised. Finding ways to de-stress and live life more calmly helps each and every one of us to meet life's many challenges with greater composure.

Before proceeding too much further we offer a practical word. Children, by virtue of their youth and inexperience, are learning. Few have learned to express all of their feelings in consistently appropriate ways. Emotional upsets are bound to occur! When children, at home or at school, are overwhelmed by extreme feelings, this is our call to duty. It is not the time to confront them and escalate their emotional intensity by demanding immediate reform. Instead, the moment should be seen as an opportunity to teach them how to calm down and wait for the wave of intense feeling to pass before uncovering solutions or asking them to be accountable for their actions. For some, this is a long and windy path. There are no quick fixes. They are reliant on our poised modelling and a consistently composed approach.

Materials required for Lesson 9

- Name tags

- Whiteboard/butcher's paper and a marker

- Post *What's the Buzz?* group rules (located on p. 20; alternatively, they can be downloaded from www.whatsthebuzz.net.au)

- Place an outline of the lesson on the whiteboard/butcher's paper

- Prepare one set of 'Calm-down option cards' for EACH child (located in the photocopiable resources at the end of this lesson; alternatively, they can be downloaded from www.whatsthebuzz.net.au) Cut them out and arrange them into their numbered groups so children can quickly grab the cards they want during *Show me the Buzz*

- One A4-sized envelope for each student to file 'Calm-down' options into

- 'Old Maid' card game – three decks

- 'Uno' card game – three decks

- 'Donkey' card game – three decks

- 'Animal Snap' card game – three decks

- A few small common items to play 'Kim's Game', plus a small piece of paper and pencil for each child

- Organise the gold nuggets, cubes to build a friendship wall, group rule and reminder cards or a similar feedback device (see the chapter, Practical Considerations)

- Organise a small gift or a reward token for each child

- Prepare handouts for parent(s):

  - One copy of this lesson for each parent to read

  - One copy of *After the Buzz: social thinking ideas for parents* for each parent to read (section follows this lesson).

Lesson 9

Arrange participants into a social circle. Welcome them back to the second half of *What's the Buzz?* Ask who can recall the names of each participant as it may be several weeks since the group last met. Prompt and support each student's effort to do this. If there is a new student introduce them and use name tags in this lesson.

Draw everyone's attention to the group rules. Display the feedback device to encourage positive social behaviours (see section on feedback ideas in the chapter, Practical Considerations). As you introduce the idea, and have the attention of students, pick up a gold nugget, a cube, a reminder card or similar to reinforce their cooperative spirit. Explain that if successful each student may leave with a small gift.

1. What's the Buzz?

What's the Buzz? introduces students to this lesson's topic and the new set of skills to be learned. Invite students to share a time when they felt stressed because life did not work out well or was not fair. Remind them that it is impossible to control the actions of others, but there are TWO brilliant ideas that help everyone to handle life's challenges in the best way.

1   Find time to relax each day

    We call this 'calm-down time'. It is an activity you enjoy that leaves you feeling pleased, peaceful or refreshed.

2   Keep building your positive thinking

    We know that positive thinking switches helpful thinking on. It opens the mind to find the best way to fix problems.

(Write these on the whiteboard or butcher's paper)

2. Show me the Buzz

Show me the Buzz gives students the opportunity to practise and show they understand the new skill set.

Begin with students sitting in the social circle. Hand each child an A4-sized envelope. Ask them to write their name on it and label it 'my calm-down ideas'. Next, spread the group out so they are sitting around the perimeter of the room.

Explain that you will call out lots of 'calm-down' options. When they hear an idea that appeals to them they are to run and collect it and place that 'calm-down' card in their envelope. Tell them they will need to move quickly (so will you) as there are loads to work through. In the end they will have a personalised collection of ideas they can share at home, own and begin to use.

'Calm-down' options

go for a walk	weed part of the garden
take a walk to the shop	rake the leaves
jump on the trampoline	go skate boarding
go for a run	take a warm bath
take a bike ride	take a shower
cuddle or pat a pet	play with a ball outside
take the dog for a walk	punch a punching bag
dress up your dolls	eat an apple
play trucks and cars	do Pilates, Yoga or listen to a relaxation CD
lay down for a few moments and breathe deeply	go play with a ball basketball, netball, football, etc.
lie on your bed and read	throw a ball at a target over and over again
lie on your bed and listen to music	
watch television	fly your kite
make something (e.g. build with blocks, Lego or Meccano)	make something with modelling clay
	draw
do homework	get a massage
play in your cubby	play with your hobby
phone a friend and talk	play with your collection
go to a friend's house	lay on the grass in the sunshine
play a computer game	do some cooking
do some gardening	colour in
work on the vegetable patch	read a book
water the plants	watch a DVD for a while

Compliment participants on their selections. Remind them that spending a small part of each day doing one of these things will help them to feel calmer and happier.

3. Do you know the Buzz?

Do you know the Buzz? is a fast-moving question time intended to consolidate the concepts gathered in the lesson.

Let's investigate how the group is developing their *positive problem solving skills*. After all, it is the key to living a balanced life.

Arrange the group into a circle and read the following statements. Their task is to decide which are based on positive or negative thinking. If they believe the statement is a positive approach they are to put their thumbs up. If they think the statement is a negative approach they are to put their thumbs down. If they are not sure they are to place their thumbs to the side and explain the confusion. Let's play!

Statements

1   At lunch one of the kids you play with kept on poking you with their finger. It was their birthday and you knew they were excited so you ignored it.

2   It's recess time, and every time you go to talk to your friends they ignore you! You turn to them and say, 'I don't have to put up with this.' Then, you walk away.

3   Your brother or sister refuses to get off the computer, and it is your turn. You slap them over the back of their head and run off to Mum to tell on them.

4   One of your friends rushes up to you and shouts, 'What you said to Dan about me was nasty. I hate you!' The truth is, you didn't say anything to Dan. You say, 'Hey, we need to talk I haven't seen Dan.'

5   Your best friend has started playing with someone who is mean to you. Later, you say to them, 'I don't want you to be friends with them anymore. You're my friend. Not theirs.'

6   Two girls roll their eyes at you to show what you are saying to the class is boring. You stare at them and say, 'That's all I need to say.'

7   When you arrive home you notice that your father is home early and has been crying. You don't say anything at all.

8   When you arrive home you notice that your father is home early and has been crying. You don't say anything at first, but later in the evening you ask him if he's okay.

9   Your homework looks hard, so you make a deal with yourself. You'll have a go at it, but not spend too much time on it.

10   'You're a retard!' is what Sam heard from a few kids every time there was a disagreement. This time Sam decided to hit two kids with his cricket bat.

4. The Buzz

During *The Buzz* students play games that help strengthen the skills central to the lesson. The more students are encouraged to play these, and similar games, the more opportunity they have to generalise their social thinking and social skills into their day-to-day interactions.

Poker Face (exciting for all ages)

Choose someone to be 'it' and ask them to stand in the middle of the social circle. All other players stand up, remaining in the circle formation. On 'go' players in the circle will walk in a clockwise direction trying to make 'it' smile or laugh – 'it' has to keep a poker face! Players in the circle must remain as a circle, may not touch 'it' and can only make 'it' laugh by using funny voices, funny faces, funny movements or telling funny jokes.

Card Games

We find it best to use two decks of cards for a group of five or six students, and three decks for a group of seven or eight students. All the card games are easy to play and come with instructions. We usually play as a whole group.

- Old Maid (passive for all ages)

- Uno (passive for older students)

- Donkey (passive for all ages)

- Animal Snap (passive for younger students)

'Good Morning Mr. President' (passive for all ages)

Each student gets the chance to sit in 'the President's chair' and be the President. This person in the chair faces away from the group. Very quietly select a student who will disguise their voice to say, 'Good morning Mr. President.' The student playing the President attempts to guess whose voice it is. If they guess correctly, they receive another turn at being the President. If they do not guess correctly the President exchanges seats with the person who disguised their voice successfully.

Kim's Game (passive for all ages)

This is a great memory game! Place between six and a dozen small items such as a pencil, paper clip, watch, book, shoe, an apple, stapler, toy car, etc. on a tray. For older students increase the number of items. Cover with a cloth. Next, sit everyone in the social circle. Place the tray in the middle of the circle and remove the cloth for one minute. At this point students (either individually or in pairs) try to remember the objects on the tray. When one minute has lapsed cover the items on the tray again. Ask each student (or pair) to list the items on a small piece of paper, but keep what they write hidden from others. The idea is to record all the items on the tray.

5. *Goodbye Buzz*

Bid students a warm goodbye and remind them to take their folders, which contain:

- a copy of this lesson for parents

- a copy of *After the Buzz: social thinking ideas for parents*

- their personalised selection of 'Calm-down option cards' to share at home.

As feedback for thoughtful behaviours each student may leave with a small gift.

After the Buzz: social thinking ideas for parents

Lesson 9: Feelings and Ideas to Create Well-Being

The purpose of this lesson was to alert your child that there are things they can do to take care of their emotional health. The lesson offered them a collection of ideas to manage the stresses within their lives more effectively so they feel calmer, happier and more resilient. Be sure to follow up on your child's selection of 'calm-down' ideas because as children become actively involved in managing their well-being the risk of them storing frustrations and exploding when least expected is minimised. Here are a few useful ideas to support your child's well-being.

- Accept that this is hard

  The truth is that learning to manage our emotions is probably one of the hardest things we ever have to learn. Do you doubt this? Think about a time when you have felt angry, upset or hurt. Were you able to stop, count to ten and think through a constructive plan of action? If honest, most admit to having had a moment or two when rational thinking went out the window. At times the strength of our emotion has driven each of us to do things we have later regretted. When looking at the management of feelings in this context it is not reasonable to expect a child, with only a few years of experience, to do what has taken us many years to refine. Then, add to the equation your child's poor social awareness, social awkwardness, low confidence, impulsiveness, or a hostile peer environment, and a considered coping style is very difficult for them to manufacture. When something goes wrong they will not naturally stop and think first – they react!

- Model what you want

  One of the best things we can do is to consistently show our children how to handle their feelings by handling ours as well as we can. When we feel upset and say nasty things about others or play the righteous role our children watch and, over the years, they learn to do the same. Never underestimate your influence.

- Read the signs and prepare!

  Try to interpret your child's frustration as a genuine emotion that should be dealt with respectfully. Set up ways, whether it is a signal or phrase, that permits them to escape a situation with dignity before their emotion boils over. For example, when you see your child becoming agitated at a family gathering you might say, 'Hey, Slade, can you help me get those things from the car?'

This prearranged question allows your child to leave the group with dignity and take a few moments with you to find their composure.

- Teach the 'Sunshine shower'

Try this approach . . .

> *'There will be times when you need to stop, gather your thoughts and calm down. This is the moment to let the sunshine rescue you. Move to a spot where you can be alone for a few moments. Sit, close your eyes and be still. Turn your back so you can feel the warmth of the sun on it, and enjoy! Now recall something you like; a favourite story, a great movie, a place you enjoyed visiting, a good time you had with friends, or think about something you are looking forward to. Spend a few moments thinking about one of these so your happy thoughts help you to feel calmer. Then, return to what you were doing with a plan to make things better.'*

- Build a guided meditation into the day

Just as adults do, children can find improved emotional steadiness by spending ten to fifteen minutes each day immersed in a guided meditation or similar. Experiment with the meditation below and if your child finds it appealing try your local library, CD outlet or the web for more. Here are a few of our favourites:

- Donna Attard. *Meditation for Children* (www.newworldmusic.com)

- Michelle Robertson–Jones. *Faerie Guided Meditations for Children* (www.paradisemusic.co.uk)

- Michelle Robertson–Jones. *Bedtime Meditations for Children* (www.paradisemusic.co.uk)

- Elizabeth Bayer and Toni Carmine Salenio. *Meditations for Children* (www.tonicarminesalenio.com)

- Crystal Rainbow Pty Ltd. *Joy – Imagination Journey for Kids* (www.crystalrainbow.com.au)

- Crystal Rainbow Pty Ltd. *Making Rainbows – Imagination Journey for Kids* (www.crystalrainbow.com.au)

- Julie Pappas. *Peaceful Journeys for Little Souls* (www.childrensmeditations.net)

- Indigo Kids Publishing. *Meditations for Children* (www.joshuabooks.com)

Try this relaxation exercise with your child.

Turn off the lights and partly draw the curtains. Ambience is important. Have your child lie on their back on the floor or bed. Begin reading to your child when ready.

> *Wriggle a bit to get comfortable.*

> *Get ready to recharge your batteries.*

After the Buzz . . . Lesson 9

Begin by thinking about something that has been hard or unfair for you today. Something that made you feel disappointed, angry or annoyed.

(Wait for a few moments)

What we are about to do will help you let go of any bad feelings you might be carrying.

Be still.

Feel your body relaxing into the bed/floor.

Start by feeling your breathing.

Place your hands on your tummy and get ready to feel it rise as you breathe in.

Take a deep breath in as I count to three.

One, two, three. Hold it in.

Begin to let it out as I count to three. One, two, three.

Feel your tummy gradually sink as you breathe out.

Slowly breathe in again. One, two, three, and hold the new air and its energy (wait).

Breathe out slowly as I count to three. Out go the angry or unfair feelings.

Wait for a bit.

Breathe in counting to three.

Wait.

Breathe out counting to three.

Keep breathing, in and out. I'll let you know when to stop (continue for a minute or two and gently place your hands on your child's hands).

Little by little parts of your body will begin to relax.

Stretch out, keeping your back and legs on the floor.

Make yourself as long as you can. Hold the stretch (pause). Let it go and relax.

Now do the same with your right leg. Tense the muscles. Hold them tight (pause). Let the muscles relax.

Do the same to the left leg now. Stretch and tighten the leg, hold it (pause). Let go.

Go to your feet. Right foot first. Wiggle your toes. Now push your toes wide apart. Hold the stretch (pause). Now relax them.

Let's do the left foot . . . wiggle your toes and push them wide apart. Hold the stretch (pause). Then relax them.

Stop for a moment and check your breathing. Keep to the rhythm. Breathing in one, two, three. Holding it for a moment. Slowly breathing out one, two, three.

Let the feeling of relaxation gently move from your legs, up your back and arms, and down into your fingers.

Place your arms by your side.

Stretch your fingers wide apart, and hold them apart while you count . . . one, two, three . . . relax them.

Do the same for your shoulders. Move your thoughts to your face. Close your eyes. Squeeze them tight. Let them relax. Do it again if you want.

Relax your facial muscles because they've been talking and smiling all day. Then tighten your face again. Keep it tight to the count of three. Relax your face again.

Now tell your mind to relax (pause). You can use what we have just done whenever you want to slow down and clear your mind.

Keep your eyes closed if you want and I'll read a short story to you.

- The groundwork counts

Find time to discuss your child's selection of 'calm-down' ideas with them. By spending a small part of most afternoons or evenings on one of the calming ideas presented in this lesson, children are far more likely to feel and act more resiliently. When the 'groundwork' of daily stress management is in place children tend to cope better with the stresses and strains of life. This really is when the investment in learning stress management pays off.

- Dealing with anger

Sometimes, children become stuck at becoming angry to get their way. They become expert at exploding and threatening because they believe it works for them. Gradually, over time, defuse anger as their favoured way to manage frustration. In happier times, discuss why they choose to explode. Most children say how terrible they feel after their angry explosion. It is not what they want and having an audience, even a caring one, can intensify the outburst.

Build practical strategies for them to cope with anger, and when they use them, praise your child! A good idea is to find a way they can transfer the angry emotional surge into the physical. Depending on the temperament and age of your child you might suggest they:

- go somewhere quiet

- punch a punching bag

- punch or twist an old cushion or pillow

- take a deep breath

- walk away

- take a shower

- twist a towel tightly

After the Buzz . . . Lesson 9

143

- bounce on the trampoline

- bite into an apple (and eat it)

- take a walk

- go for a jog or a run

- go to a friend's house

- sit outside and look at the sky

- lie under a tree and watch the leaves move in the breeze

- draw a picture of the person who you are annoyed with and tear it into little bits

- write an angry letter then rip it up

- rip up a newspaper or magazine

- rip up a kitchen sponge into a thousand pieces

- run up and down a staircase

- throw a ball at a target over and over again

- go and kick a ball

- listen to music

- go to the bedroom and scream into the pillow

- phone a friend, anyone trustworthy, and complain.

The best outcomes occur when children latch on to a particular strategy, and routinely use it. Getting into a habit embeds the new behaviour and soon it becomes automatic.

• A golden rule

When your child becomes upset or angry always offer a sensible way they can calm themselves. When their feelings are out of control and it is too difficult for them to think clearly or talk rationally make it a rule to not participate. Quietly move away and give them time to recover. Wait for them to gather some emotional control before trying to problem solve with them.

Photocopiable resources now follow, and don't forget the online resources at www.whatsthebuzz.net.au!

What's the Buzz?

Calm-down option cards

What's the Buzz? Calm-down option 1 **Go for a Walk**	
What's the Buzz? Calm-down option 2 **Take a Walk to the Shop**	
What's the Buzz? Calm-down option 3 **Jump on the Trampoline**	
What's the Buzz? Calm-down option 4 **Go for a Run**	
What's the Buzz? Calm-down option 5 **Take a Bike Ride**	
What's the Buzz? Calm-down option 6 **Cuddle or Pat a Pet**	
What's the Buzz? Calm-down option 7 **Take the Dog for a Walk**	
What's the Buzz? Calm-down option 8 **Dress up your Dolls**	

What's the Buzz?

Calm-down option cards *continued . . .*

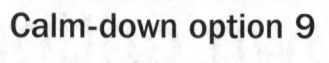

What's the Buzz? Calm-down option 9 **Play Trucks and Cars**	

What's the Buzz? Calm-down option 10 **Lay Down for a few Moments and Breathe Deeply**	

What's the Buzz? Calm-down option 11 **Lie on your Bed and Read**	

What's the Buzz? Calm-down option 12 **Lie on your Bed and Listen to Music**	

What's the Buzz? Calm-down option 13 **Watch Television**	

What's the Buzz? Calm-down option 14 **Make Something (e.g. Build with Blocks, Lego or Meccano)**	

What's the Buzz? Calm-down option 15 **Do Homework**	

What's the Buzz? Calm-down option 16 **Play in your Cubby**	

What's the Buzz? Calm-down option 17 **Phone a Friend and Talk**	

What's the Buzz?

Calm-down option cards *continued . . .*

| *What's the Buzz?* | Calm-down option 18 |  |

Go to a Friend's House

| *What's the Buzz?* | Calm-down option 19 |

Play a Computer Game

| *What's the Buzz?* | Calm-down option 20 |

Do some Gardening

| *What's the Buzz?* | Calm-down option 21 |

Work on the Vegetable Patch

| *What's the Buzz?* | Calm-down option 22 |

Water the Plants

| *What's the Buzz?* | Calm-down option 23 |

Weed Part of the Garden

| *What's the Buzz?* | Calm-down option 24 |

Rake the Leaves

| *What's the Buzz?* | Calm-down option 25 |

Go Skate Boarding

| *What's the Buzz?* | Calm-down option 26 |

Take a Warm Bath

What's the Buzz?

Calm-down option cards *continued . . .*

What's the Buzz?   Calm-down option 27

Take a Shower

What's the Buzz?   Calm-down option 28

Play with a Ball Outside

What's the Buzz?   Calm-down option 29

Punch a Punching Bag

What's the Buzz?   Calm-down option 30

Eat an Apple

What's the Buzz?   Calm-down option 31

Do Pilates, Yoga or Listen to a Relaxation CD

What's the Buzz?   Calm-down option 32

Go Play with a Ball Basketball, Netball, Football, etc.

What's the Buzz?   Calm-down option 33

Throw a Ball at a Target Over and Over Again

What's the Buzz?   Calm-down option 34

Fly your Kite

What's the Buzz?   Calm-down option 35

Make Something with Modelling Clay

What's the Buzz?

Calm-down option cards *continued . . .*

What's the Buzz? Calm-down option 36 ### Draw	

What's the Buzz? Calm-down option 37 ### Get a Massage	

What's the Buzz? Calm-down option 38 ### Play with your Hobby	

What's the Buzz? Calm-down option 39 ### Play with your Collection	

What's the Buzz? Calm-down option 40 ### Lay on the Grass in the Sunshine	

What's the Buzz? Calm-down option 41 ### Do some Cooking	

What's the Buzz? Calm-down option 42 ### Colour in	

What's the Buzz? Calm-down option 43 ### Read a Book	

What's the Buzz? Calm-down option 44 ### Watch a DVD for a While	

Empathy, Responding to Others

Explanation

Many young people participating in *What's the Buzz?* struggle to keep their own emotions in check, so meeting the emotional needs of others is often tricky, and requires new levels of social thinking. Not only is it hard for them to interpret the countless emotional messages embedded in language, but reading fleeting and variable non-verbal exchanges accurately is problematic. Living with social blindness or clumsiness places our target group at a great disadvantage compared to their more socially accomplished peers.

This lesson examines how to read the emotional needs of others and respond to them more empathically. To do this, two processes must occur. The first is to acknowledge how the other person is feeling. This validates what they are experiencing and reassures them they are cared for. Second, something should be said that eases that person's difficulty, or allows them to see there is a possible solution. In other words, the aim is to help them feel better.

Empathy and compassion are two highly prized qualities in the social world. They are prerequisites for building and preserving relationships. So let us follow the idea that when an individual is able to show empathy – give the right look, provide the right words and show a compassionate response – they should in fact pass one of the key criteria of friendship with flying colours.

Materials required for Lesson 10

- Whiteboard/butcher's paper and a marker

- Post *What's the Buzz?* group rules (located on p. 20; alternatively, they can be downloaded from www.whatsthebuzz.net.au)

- Place an outline of the lesson on the whiteboard/butcher's paper

- Photocopy 'Role-play cards, empathy' (located in the photocopiable resources at the end of this lesson; alternatively, they can be downloaded from www.whatsthebuzz.net.au)

- Four sheets of large format graph paper for the game 'Boxes'

- Eight pencils or markers

- Organise the gold nuggets, cubes to build a friendship wall, group rule and reminder cards or a similar feedback device (see the chapter, Practical Considerations)

- Organise a small gift or a reward token for each child

- Prepare handouts for parent(s):

  - One copy of this lesson for each parent to read

  - One copy of *After the Buzz: social thinking ideas for parents* for each parent to read (section follows this lesson).

Lesson 10

Arrange participants into a social circle. Welcome them.

Draw everyone's attention to the group rules. Display the feedback device to encourage positive social behaviours (see section on feedback ideas in the chapter, Practical Considerations). As you introduce the idea, and have the attention of students, pick up a gold nugget, a cube, a reminder card or similar to reinforce their cooperative spirit. Explain that if successful each student may leave with a small gift.

1. What's the Buzz?

What's the Buzz? introduces students to this lesson's topic and the new set of skills to be learned. Explain that when someone expresses a thought or a feeling the best rule is to treat them with respect.

It does not matter whether their thought or feeling is different from ours – it is important to that person.

The best way to respond is to show empathy: care, kindness and a positive attitude. To do this say something that will help them feel better, especially if they are hurt or upset. This means that you look as if you understand and care.

An example:

> Your friend has lost their drawing book and they are getting very upset. You could say, 'That's really annoying to lose your favourite book. I can understand why you are so cross. Would you like me to help you look for it? Maybe I could ask the others if they have seen it.'

To show empathy do two things:

1 Say something that shows you understand how they must be feeling.

2 Do or say something to comfort them, or gives hope.

This is how empathy works; it is expected and appreciated by others.

(Write the 'TWO behaviours that show empathy' on the whiteboard or butcher's paper for students to refer to)

2. Show me the Buzz

Show me the Buzz gives students the opportunity to practise and show they understand the new skill set. To begin, let's start with a role-play.

Role-play example

> Student volunteer: 'I'm really worried about my mum. You know, she's been sick for a long time now and I think she's getting worse.'
>
> *Facilitator THINKS (say this out loud so students hear the thinking processes): his/her mother has been sick for a long time. Things seem to be getting worse. This sounds very bad to me.*
>
> Facilitator SAYS to the volunteer: 'I'm really so sorry to hear that. It's been tough on you. I think your mum is very lucky to have you. Is there anything I could do to help?'

Next, arrange the students into a social circle. Ask each to take a 'Role-play card' from you. Call two students up at a time. One of the students will read a 'Role-play card' to the other. The student who listens will then try to respond showing empathy. Remind participants to use the TWO empathic behaviours written on the whiteboard or butcher's paper.

Once the student has responded allow the group to comment on the quality of their response. Also, ask them to share what they were thinking, but chose NOT to say. Next, ask them to swap roles, and progressively give each group member a turn.

Role-play cards: empathy

1   'I failed my math test. I know I didn't study. My parents will kill me!'

2   'Blah, blah, blah he goes! My dad is always telling me what to do.'

3   'Look at my hair. Mum made me get it cut. It looks stupid. I feel horrible.'

4   'I can't find my science project anywhere! I'm dead!'

5   'The teacher didn't give one to me in the game. She gave lollies to others. She's not fair.'

6   'I feel horrible. A lot of kids don't like me you know.'

7   'It's not fair, my sister is much better at swimming than me and wins all of the competitions.'

8   'That kid keeps picking on me.'

9   'My teacher is always yelling at me for talking.'

10   'My teacher wrote that I'm disruptive. My parents are mad at me. It's not fair.'

11   'I don't want to do sports day. Everyone sees how bad I am. I hope it rains!'

12   'The Principal told Mum that if I'm not better behaved I'll have to leave.'

The use of empathy is one of the best ways to strengthen friendships and start new ones!

3. Do you know the Buzz?

Do you know the Buzz? is a quick question time. Its intention is to consolidate the ideas gathered in the lesson so far. Encourage everyone to have a go.

The challenge is to decide which statements are empathic. Ask students to put their thumbs up if they hear a thoughtful or caring response, and thumbs down to indicate unkind or poor responses. If they believe it is too hard to tell they are to put their thumbs to the side. When challenged they must be prepared to explain their decision. Let's play!

Round 1

Statements

1 Your brother comes home upset because his soccer team lost again. You stop what you are doing and say, 'Hey, Brett, you can't win them all. I know you would have done your best.'

2 Your brother comes home upset because his soccer team lost again. You continue to play on the computer and say, 'Hey, Brett, well done!'

3 Your five-year-old sister can't find her favourite doll. You tell her not to worry too much because it's time she grew up.

4 Your mum comes home from work exhausted and says, 'I feel way too tired to cook dinner so I've ordered pizza.' You say, 'But, Mum, this morning you said we'd have chicken nuggets and I want them!'

5 Your dad is home sick from work. You want him to fix your bike, but he can hardly move because he's feeling so terrible. You tell him how frustrated you are about your bike, but say the most important thing is for him to get better.

6 Your dad arrives home and looks sad. He tells everyone he's got a big problem at work and doesn't know what to do. You say, 'Cheer up Dad. You're good at what you do. You'll think of something. Just take it easy and have fun at home with us!'

7 One of the kids in your class keeps hanging around your group. He's okay. You can tell he wants to join in. You turn to him and say, 'Sorry, but we've got all the players we need.'

8 Earlier, you watched two of your friends have a fight. Later one comes to you and asks you to take their side. You say, 'I bet you're feeling awful. I can't take sides, but I will sit with you both while you sort it out.'

4. The Buzz

During *The Buzz* students play games that help them to practise their newly learned skills.

Who Is It? (passive for all ages)

Ask group members to close their eyes, bend over, place their heads in their laps, and listen carefully. Explain that you will describe three features of a student in the group. You might say, 'This person (without naming them) has black hair, is tall and has a wonderful smile.'

As the students think they know who the mystery person is they sit up and put their hand up ready to be asked. If the group begins to struggle, throw in an additional clue. An interesting addition to this game is to include clues about what the person likes, does, is known for or should be known for. This is an engaging way for students to receive feedback about how others see them and to find out more about one another.

Boxes (passive for older students)

Boxes is a simple game where players are required to read the play and think ahead. It's age old and enjoys the same reputation as 'Noughts and Crosses'.

To play 'Boxes' provide each pair of students with a large format piece of graph paper to share, and a pencil each. To prepare the game students will need to mark dots on intersecting lines so they end up with a rectangular collection of dots, say four lots of eight rows.

To begin, one player draws a short vertical or horizontal line between any two dots (no diagonal lines are permitted). The next player must do the same, but the question is where will they draw it? They may choose to connect to their opponent's line and extend it to the next dot, or continue from it at right angles. They may even choose to begin a new line somewhere else on the grid.

The aim of the game is to make the fourth side on as many squares as possible and claim that box as theirs. Once they claim a box they write the letter of their Christian name inside it, and must take a free turn. Free turns are a bonus at the outset, but a curse later in the game. And, so the game continues until every square has been claimed. Each player counts how many squares they have won, and the person who claimed the most wins.

Remind participants that this game gives them a chance to practise the WINNING recipe learned earlier in the programme. That is, when you play for fun, you might win or lose, but it is your *friendly behaviours* that will encourage others to like you and want to play with you again.

Silly Sally/Silly Sam (passive for all ages)

Have participants sit in a social circle. Sit yourself in the middle of the circle and explain that you are 'Silly Sally' or 'Silly Sam' and that you have a very unusual rule. The only way that anyone in the group can join is if they can guess the very special rule in your head.

To start with Silly Sally/Silly Sam only likes things that have 'double letters' in them. Do not say this to the group, instead, say . . . 'Silly Sally/Silly Sam likes soccer, but doesn't like golf. Silly Sally/Silly Sam likes apples but doesn't like beans, Silly Sally/Silly Sam likes green, but doesn't like red, Silly Sally/Silly Sam likes the moon, but doesn't like Mars. What is it that Silly Sally/Silly Sam really likes?'

Here is another, but this time Silly Sally/Silly Sam only likes 'collective nouns' . . . 'Silly Sally/Silly Sam likes flocks of birds, but doesn't like eagles, Silly Sally/Silly Sam likes the pride of lions, but doesn't like Leo the lion, Silly Sally/Silly Sam likes homes, but doesn't like that house, Silly Sally/Silly Sam likes people, but doesn't like that person. What is it that Silly Sally/Silly Sam really likes?'

For this last one Silly Sally/Silly Sam only likes 'big things' . . . 'Silly Sally/Silly Sam likes the Empire State building, but doesn't like houses, Silly Sally/Silly Sam likes dinosaurs, but doesn't like insects, Silly Sally/Silly Sam likes buses, but doesn't like Mini Cooper cars, Silly Sally/Silly Sam likes the Amazon river, but doesn't like the stream in the park. What is it that Silly Sally/Silly Sam really likes?'

5. Goodbye Buzz

Bid students a warm goodbye and remind them to take their folders, which contain:

- a copy of this lesson for parents

- a copy of *After the Buzz: social thinking ideas for parents*.

As feedback for thoughtful behaviours each student may leave with a small gift.

After the Buzz: social thinking ideas for parents

Lesson 10: Empathy, Responding to Others

This lesson focused on how to respond to the emotional needs of others by using empathy. Your child learned that to show empathy they need to display TWO behaviours:

1   They need to say something that shows they understand how the other person must be feeling.

2   They need to do or say something to comfort the person, or give them hope.

This is how empathy works. As empathy is a highly valued quality in the social world – it can make, repair and strengthen friendships – here are a few ideas parents may wish to use or adapt to support your child's emergence into the social world.

• Teach by example

A natural way to teach empathy to our children is for us to show empathy and compassion at every opportunity that presents itself. Our children never stop watching and learning from us!

• The art of managing our children's emotions empathetically

When your child is upset over an incident, refrain from saying, *'Hey, stop making such a big deal out of it'* or *'Why are you so upset over that?'* The more parents say *'get over it'* the more children are likely to feel not listened to. In contrast, spontaneously jumping in to find a solution for them, or spending too much time chatting about the issue, are counterproductive strategies. Both strategies steer children away from developing flexible, independent patterns of recovery. There truly is an art to managing our children's emotions empathetically. It begins with accepting that from time to time they must experience being upset or unhappy. These are real and normal feelings. The most helpful approach is to acknowledge how your child is feeling by recognising their upset or disappointment. They need to know that you are there to listen, empathise, understand and suggest, but you are not responsible for creating their happiness or solutions to their upsets.

• Teach your child how to think and live compassionately

An easy way to do this is to watch a movie together. Many movies and sitcoms are wonderful as a springboard to observe the behaviours of others. Together, play with questions such as:

- Why a character was liked?

- Why another was disliked? Did you dislike them?

- What could have they said or done to help others like them more?

- Was there a reason for them to behave like this?

- Who was their favourite character? Why? What qualities did they show that you liked?

- Who was their least favourite character? Why?

- Who was the hero? What made them a hero?

- Who was the victim? How could you tell? Was it their fault? Was it anyone's fault?

- What reasons do you have to make this judgement?

- If you had been 'so and so' what would have you done to make things better?

Observing behaviour and emotion in this way guides children to see the complexities behind human interactions. An extraordinary display of frustration, where the character expresses his emotions with overt anger and aggression, albeit humorously, is seen in Basil Fawlty in Fawlty Towers. Even after thirty years this series makes for wonderful discussion. Basil's bad temper in combination with having to be right and showing poor empathy to others causes him so much trouble.

- Play 'what if?'

To do this read the scenario below to the family.

> 'Dakota, your good friend and someone you have known for ages, has been picking on a quiet kid who is new to your class. Actually you like Jono, the new boy. He has similar interests to you and seems friendly. At first, you thought what Dakota was doing was funny, but now it's getting serious. Jono tries to stay away from Dakota, but Dakota seems to track him down and pick on him. You can see Jono is becoming more and more upset. Dakota and a few others still think it's funny.'

What could you SAY or DO to show understanding and kindness to both Dakota and Jono? Discuss this together. Remember, to respond with empathy, TWO things need to happen:

1 Something needs to be said that shows you understand how the other person must be feeling.

2 Do or say something to comfort the other person and give them hope.

- Learning to say 'sorry' matters!

Some find it difficult to say, and others throw 'sorry' about nonchalantly to excuse anything they do. Used genuinely, 'sorry' can repair so many situations. Explore what 'sorry' is about, when to use it and how it can be said sincerely. Have fun with your children role-playing situations where 'sorry' might be helpful. Try 'sorry' with a smile, a touch, a wink, a handshake, a rub on someone's arm or a hug. Coach your child to understand that saying 'sorry' isn't an admission of wrongdoing and it may not always be accepted by another. However, it is a powerful gesture to reduce resentment and allow relationships to heal and grow.

• Helping others

A practical way for your child to give pleasure to others, and see it returned, is to arrange for them to prepare a meal for the family each week or fortnight. Sure, some support may be required, but with a little help and supervision most seven-year-olds are capable of preparing a simple meal for their family. Nudging children to do more for themselves, and for others, helps children to stretch their independence and thoughtfulness.

Without wishing to upset any parent, a good number of children with memory weaknesses, social delay and behavioural immaturities often have their well-meaning mothers and fathers squarely in their service. Many become accustomed to receiving help and lose opportunities to give to others. Perhaps the next step is to steer your children to help others outside the family. The idea of giving back and doing thoughtful things for others instantly immerses them in an emotionally broader and richer world. As they see and absorb the thoughts and feelings of others a more empathic view of life is promoted. Ask yourself, how long is it since your child sent a thank-you card, a small present, a warm email, a friendly note, a hand-made card, or made a phone call to someone who has been helpful or needs their spirits raised? Start by setting them up to deliver kindnesses. Teaching children how to care underpins that they themselves are cared for.

Photocopiable resources now follow, and don't forget the online resources at www.whatsthebuzz.net.au!

After the Buzz . . . Lesson 10

What's the Buzz?
Role-play cards, empathy

What's the Buzz?	Role-play card, empathy 1

'I failed my math test. I know I didn't study. My parents will kill me!'

What's the Buzz?	Role-play card, empathy 2

'Blah, blah, blah he goes! My dad is always telling me what to do.'

What's the Buzz?	Role-play card, empathy 3

'Look at my hair. Mum made me get it cut. It looks stupid. I feel horrible.'

What's the Buzz?	Role-play card, empathy 4

'I can't find my science project anywhere! I'm dead!'

What's the Buzz?	Role-play card, empathy 5

'The teacher didn't give one to me in the game. She gave lollies to others. She's not fair.'

What's the Buzz?	Role-play card, empathy 6

'I feel horrible. A lot of kids don't like me you know.'

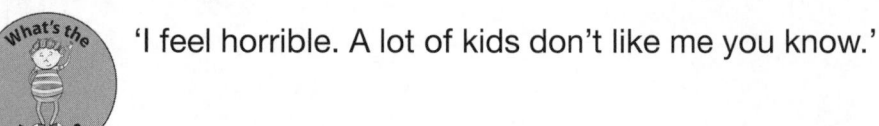

What's the Buzz?

Role-play cards, empathy

continued . . .

What's the Buzz?   Role-play card, empathy 7

 'It's not fair, my sister is much better at swimming than me and wins all of the competitions.'

What's the Buzz?   Role-play card, empathy 8

 'That kid keeps picking on me.'

What's the Buzz?   Role-play card, empathy 9

 'My teacher is always yelling at me for talking.'

What's the Buzz?   Role-play card, empathy 10

 'My teacher wrote that I'm disruptive. My parents are mad at me. It's not fair.'

What's the Buzz?   Role-play card, empathy 11

 'I don't want to do sports day. Everyone sees how bad I am. I hope it rains!'

What's the Buzz?   Role-play card, empathy 12

 'The Principal told Mum that if I'm not better behaved I'll have to leave.'

Handling Worry

Explanation

Just as we worry, children worry. Normally, it is seen as a reassuring sign that their development is on track as worry is a useful means to plan, sort, prioritise, unravel problems and cope with life's experiences.

Worry, however, can become a problem when it is ever present and affects one's ability to participate freely in life. Incessant worry thwarts the happiness we usually gain from being with others. In addition, it limits concentration, memory, academic performance, and invites disturbing thoughts that can actually produce signs of physical sickness. It even plays with our ability to fall asleep peacefully and stay asleep throughout the night.

Children tend to fall into one of three categories. Some rarely worry. Most live comfortably with low level worries, and the rest carry a more natural disposition that invites worry. The worriers worry about almost everything: who they should play with, whether they are liked, why their knees are knobbly, when they might stop growing, why Dad ran late, whether loved ones will die, the chances of their house being robbed or burned, what the new food in their lunch box will taste like or whether they will pass the dreaded weekly maths or spelling test. Such worriers worry from the moment they wake up to the moment they drift off into a fitful sleep at night. The intensity of their worry is beyond what most consider healthy.

Too much worry too often is a serious problem. We now know that when children are stressed by extreme circumstances and uncertainty for too long their brains switch to permanent high alert. To sustain this state a stress hormone called cortisol is released by the adrenal gland to increase blood pressure and blood sugar. As this hormone circulates in the brain it cuts access to the rational, thinking, memory and immune system parts of the brain. For a child who is constantly anxious or continually stressed their decision making becomes trapped in the emotional part of the brain so every new experience is perceived as a threat and dealt with as a threat. As the brain continues to grow the wiring to the rational, thinking, memory and immune system doesn't set up as strongly and a lot of the action is switched to the emotional part of the brain. The link between children who carry too much stress or worry in their life and the likelihood of serious anxiety disorders and depression is now well established (Stanley, 2008). Children who fall into this category require thoughtful professional support: a school counsellor, a psychologist, a paediatrician, a psychiatrist, a social worker or someone linked to a local community health centre.

In this lesson our focus is twofold. First, to teach students that worrying, providing it is within healthy parameters, is normal as it helps us to make sense of our world. Second, most of us do much better when we learn to understand our worry patterns and work with them to resolve problems. We will do this by equipping children with a few practical strategies to calm themselves when feeling too anxious or worried.

Materials required for Lesson 11

- Whiteboard/butcher's paper and a marker

- Post *What's the Buzz?* group rules (located on p. 20; alternatively, they can be downloaded from www.whatsthebuzz.net.au)

- Place an outline of the lesson on the whiteboard/butcher's paper

- Pencils and coloured markers to share between students to draw 'Worry bugs'

- Photocopy two copies of 'Worry bug, worksheet' per student (located in the photocopiable resources at the end of this lesson; alternatively, they can be downloaded from www.whatsthebuzz.net.au)

- Photocopy one copy of 'Worry, my catastrophe scale' per student (located in the photocopiable resources at the end of this lesson; alternatively, they can be downloaded from www.whatsthebuzz.net.au)

- Four blindfolds on hand to play the game 'Walking and Talking'

- One roll of masking tape to play the game 'Bobsledding'

- Organise the gold nuggets, cubes to build a friendship wall, group rule and reminder cards or a similar feedback device (see the chapter, Practical Considerations)

- Organise a small gift or a reward token for each child

- Prepare handouts for parent(s):

  - One copy of this lesson for each parent to read

  - One copy of *After the Buzz: social thinking ideas for parents* for each parent to read (section follows this lesson).

Lesson 11

Arrange participants into a social circle. Welcome them. Draw everyone's attention to the group rules. Display the feedback device to encourage positive social behaviours. Explain that if successful each student may leave with a small gift.

1. What's the Buzz?

What's the Buzz? introduces students to the new set of skills to help them deal with their worries.

Explain to your students that worrying is normal. Almost everyone does it. Worry can help us solve upsetting situations and prepare us to cope with risks. But, worry becomes a problem when we do it too often or begin to worry about things that are not really risky. Too much worry can make it hard for us to learn, play, be friendly and sleep.

One way to deal with our worries is to see them as annoying little 'worry bugs'.

Worry bugs

These are NOT real bugs, but an idea we can use to deal with our worries. Think about this: when someone has a cold they might say, 'I feel miserable. I've caught a bug.' Their bug is really a tiny germ and until their body kills it they feel unwell. In the meantime, they might distract themselves by watching a movie or playing with their DS. If all they did was to lie on the couch thinking about how sick they felt they would probably feel much worse!

In the same way, if we choose to let that annoying little 'worry bug' run madly around our minds we will start to feel more and more worried about things. Don't panic. We can control them, and with practice get rid of them. After all a worry is only a thought and we are in charge of our thoughts! Here are a few ideas to fight off your 'worry bugs':

- Think: how serious is this worry? Train yourself to use a 'Worry, my catastrophe scale' (show the 'Worry, my catastrophe scale' to the students). Briefly explain that by rating a worry on the scale the worry stays as real as it should be.

- Use positive thinking such as, 'you're not going to get me worry bug', or 'I've been vaccinated', or 'go pick on someone else' or 'go away worry bug, I'm bigger than you'. Sometimes saying this out loud is helpful. Train your mind to switch to happy thoughts and stay with them by getting up, walking away and doing something that makes you feel happier.

- Imagine clever weapons like laser beams that shoot from the back of your eyes sizzling any 'worry bug' that comes your way. Set your laser beams to automatic so you don't have to think about them.

- Give yourself permission to worry just once a day, and make it at a time that suits you! Perhaps after school when you can talk to someone about it.

- A great idea is to make a worry book or worry box. Write your worries in the book or place them in the box. Then, pass them on to a parent or teacher who becomes the 'keeper' of the worries and takes care of them while you're able to get on enjoying your life.

These five ideas to fight the 'worry bugs' always resonate well with children. If time permits ask the group to come up with their own ideas. They'll have some fabulously convoluted ideas!

2. Show me the Buzz

Show me the Buzz gives students the opportunity to practise and show they understand the new skill set.

Provide each student with a 'Worry bug, worksheet' and have plenty of coloured pencils or markers to share. Encourage students to use their imagination and draw the image of their very own 'worry bug'. Inspire students to add thought bubbles and speech captions to their 'worry bugs' such as:

- *'I make her worry that no one likes her.'*

- *'I make him worry that he's dumb.'*

- *'I make him so nervous he can't think straight.'*

- *'I make her worry that she'll never grow.'*

The bugs that group members create will become the 'worry bugs' they visualise every time a worry creeps into their mind. It is the bug they will shrink, ignore or sizzle away with the powerful lasers in the back of their eyes. Display the worry bugs around the room after completion and discuss them. Make sure you do one yourself!

3. Do you know the Buzz?

Do you know the Buzz? is a quick question time. It consolidates the ideas gathered in the lesson so far. Arrange the group into a social circle and encourage everyone to have a go. Keep it quick!

Round 1

Hand each student a 'Worry, my catastrophe scale'. The task is for them to rate each of the worries below with a number from the scale. Students can indicate this by holding the 'Worry, my catastrophe scale' up to their chest and pointing to the intensity of the worry.

- You're at school and have forgotten your lunch.

- You have an itch on your foot.

- You have to move house, leave your friends and start at a new school.

- You cannot find your DS anywhere.

- You have lost your DS in your bed.

- You have to go to the school camp.

- Your dog is very, very sick.

- Mum forgot to give you your pocket money yesterday.

- Your grandfather is seriously ill.

- You didn't get invited to a friend's birthday party.

Provide an opportunity to discuss variations in ratings and why these occur.

Round 2

Ask students to solve each worry with one constructive thought.

- 'What if she's horrible to me again today?'

- 'What if I catch a cold before the soccer match on Saturday?'

- 'What if Mum says, "I want you to stay at home alone for half an hour?" I hate that.'

- 'What if I have to repeat a year at school?'

- 'What if Mum doesn't come to camp with me? I'll really worry!'

- 'What if I can't do my homework?'

- 'What if Dad gets really angry again tonight?'

- 'What if we have to move house?'

4. The Buzz

During *The Buzz* students play games that help them to practise their newly learned skills.

Walking and Talking (passive for all ages)

This activity involves clear communication and trust. In fact, establishing a caring tone is essential. Divide the group into pairs. One partner is blindfolded and the other becomes their eyes. It is wise to explain that it is normal to feel a little worried about placing your faith in another person like this, and the person you are placing your trust in carries a big responsibility.

'Walking and talking' is best played outside. Point out the boundaries and any unsafe obstacles you would like players to stay away from. In this game one of the partners leads their blindfolded counterpart around the area ensuring they do not bump into obstacles or hurt themselves. They can try to do this with or without holding hands. Holding hands is a sensible idea for younger children. The object is for the person who is the 'eyes' to give clear, helpful instructions in order to get their partner safely back home. There is no time limit. Once players have completed a circuit around the area they can swap roles.

Wink Murder (exciting for older students)

Choose a detective from the group and ask them to leave the room for a few moments. The group needs to be very quiet. Next, choose a murderer from the group. The detective returns and stands in the middle of the circle. The murderer secretly winks at members of the group. This unfolds fairly slowly and as group members receive the wink from the murderer they fall to the ground and die. It is fine for the person dying to be very dramatic. The detective's task is to find the winking murderer before too many group members are killed off.

Bobsledding (exciting for all ages)

This is a team game. Try to make the teams even. Aim at teams of two, three or four. Each team sits on the floor in a line, one person behind the other. Next, each team member wraps their legs around the waist of the person in front of them and squeezes firmly. To create a finishing line place a piece of masking tape on the floor about 5 metres from the start position. On 'go', teams may only use their hands on the floor to slide their way to the end. If a team breaks apart, they must go back to the start together before they continue. The first team with every member over the finish line wins! Children of all ages love slightly extended versions of this so they can have points and experience a grand final play off.

5. Goodbye Buzz

Bid students a warm goodbye and remind them to take their folders, which contain:

- a copy of this lesson for parents

- a copy of *After the Buzz: social thinking ideas for parents*

- the completed 'Worry bug, worksheet' and a spare blank one

- a copy of 'Worry, my catastrophe scale'.

As feedback for thoughtful behaviours each student may leave with a small gift.

After the Buzz: social thinking ideas for parents

Lesson 11: Handling Worry

In this lesson your child learned that worrying, in the main, is normal because it helps us to make sense of our world. Your child also learned that most of us do much better when we learn to understand our worry patterns and work with them to fix the problems driving them. Here are a number of sensible ideas parents can use at home to reduce their children's susceptibility to worry and anxiousness.

- What's happening at home?

  It is fair to say that a few children are predisposed to worry. They are our 'natural born worriers'. Beyond this, a sensible beginning point is to assess the influences occurring within your family: a separation, a divorce, arguments, financial difficulties, racial taunts, recovery following a car accident, a sick family member, even a story aired on the evening news can trigger feelings of distress, dread and helplessness.

- Get to know their worries

  Do you know what your child worries about? Is there a recurring theme? Do their worries concern self-esteem, perfectionism, separation, fear, death or are they related to social encounters. Once you know then it is possible to teach specific strategies to work with.

- Be the best role model

  Let your children see you logically talk your way through worries and problems. Whenever you can, allow them to witness you using positive self-talk and positive thinking to find solutions. As we 'talk it out loud' the logical order of what can be done enhances our motivation and chances of success. Show your children how they can also rely on this. Let them hear you say, 'I know I can deal with this. I need to think about it. First, I'll. . .'

- Make time to talk about the highs and lows of the day

  Many parents gently, but deliberately build this time into evening meal conversations. It is a perfect forum to share successes and discuss troubles that may have arisen during the day.

- Always deal with worries in the daytime!

  Why? You know what it is like; in the gloominess of dark at bedtime everything seems at its very worst and positive thoughts are hard to gather.

A useful way to help your child deal with worry is to get them to draw it, along with ideas to deal with it. Then, get them to place it into their worry tin. It's just a matter of buying a small tin with a slot in the lid. For extra security, so the worries can't possibly escape, you might buy a tin with a tiny padlock on the lid. Once the worry has been discussed, drawn, written, and folded up into the slotted tin it doesn't need any further energy spent on it. The fascinating part is that when the worries are looked at weeks later most children will say, 'Those worries are pathetic now!' This in itself delivers a healthy message about how much value we should give to worrying. As most of us have learned over the years so few of our worries actually come to fruition. Using a worry tin in this way is a powerful teacher of this for children.

- Empower your child

Remind them that worries are thoughts within their control.

In this lesson, we purposely used the term 'worry bugs'. Our suggestion is for you to draw your own 'worry bug' for your child to see. Incorporate thought bubbles and speech captions just as your child did in the lesson. Share how you deal with your worries and be sure to ask about the 'Worry scale' in their folder. Might this be something to be used at home?

- Always use a logical 3-step plan to minimise worry

1 Work out how serious it is

Use a worry scale similar to the one your child has brought home from this lesson. Ask your child to rate their worry anywhere between 1 and 5, with 1 being a slight setback and 5 being an irreversible disaster. So often worriers tend to catastrophise and think the worry is much, much worse than it really is. Rating the worry helps to keep it in perspective.

2 Gently challenge their worried thinking

Ask logical and realistic questions such as: 'Well, what usually happens?' 'What is most likely to happen?' 'What plans can be made to deal with it?' By consistently using this logical approach children learn that the worry is not very likely, and contingency plans can always be made. Realistic thinking replaces frightened thinking, and as it does your child can effectively begin to problem solve.

3 Teach your child to switch worried thoughts to happy ones

Train them to tell their worry that they are stronger than it, and it will never beat them, even if they have to say it out loud! Switch to a happy thought and to stay with it teach them to get up, walk away and do something that makes them feel happy.

- The problem of too much reassurance

It is vital to reassure children that they are safe and you understand their worries. However, when we talk too intensely about a child's worries, dissect and rehash them this can unintentionally leave the child with the impression

After the Buzz . . . Lesson 11

that there must be something very serious to worry about. Be watchful of striking a healthy balance between being supportive and offering too much helpful talk.

- Get a worry doll

  OXFAM, the international aid organisation, sells 'Guatemalan worry dolls' in many cities around the world. These dolls are crafted around the image of Guatemalan children wearing traditional costume. The idea is the worry doll can take care of a child's worries so they can sleep peacefully. So before climbing into bed it's time for your child to tell each of their worries to the worry doll, place it under their pillow, and let the doll deal with them!

- Never forget – humour, playfulness and lightheartedness

  Well placed humour inspires a lightness that reaches a long way towards disarming worry. Never be shy about telling your child a funny or disarming story to help put things in perspective.

- A few children need a worry specialist

  Growing up is hard for some children. Sometimes they go through phases where they seem to have a bigger worry each day. Always follow your instincts as this is the time to seek expert professional support; a school counsellor, a psychologist, a paediatrician, a psychiatrist, a social worker or someone linked to a local community health centre. The influence of a skilled professional can have your child experimenting with interventions and ideas that will amaze you, and leave them feeling far more in control.

Photocopiable resources now follow, and don't forget the online resources at www.whatsthebuzz.net.au!

After the Buzz . . . Lesson 11

What's the Buzz?

Worry bug, worksheet

Name: _____

Draw your 'Worry Bug'

Add thought bubbles and speech captions to so we know how it worries you!

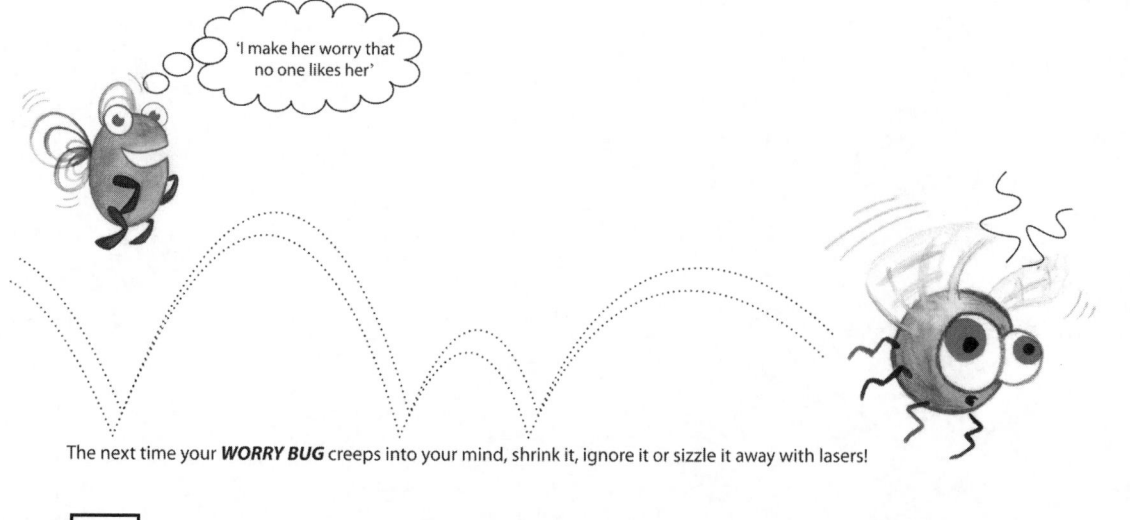

The next time your **WORRY BUG** creeps into your mind, shrink it, ignore it or sizzle it away with lasers!

What's the Buzz?

Worry, my catastrophe scale

Name: _____

Think: how serious is this worry?

Train yourself to use this scale and rate your worry.

By rating it, the worry stays as real as it should be, and you can find a solution.

MY WORRY SCALE

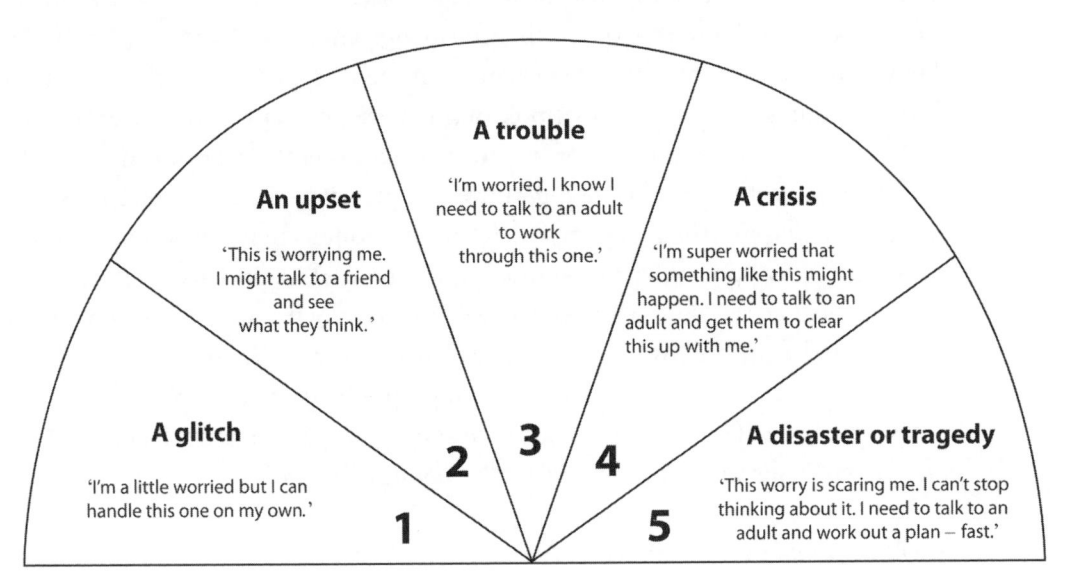

A trouble

'I'm worried. I know I need to talk to an adult to work through this one.'

An upset

'This is worrying me. I might talk to a friend and see what they think.'

A crisis

'I'm super worried that something like this might happen. I need to talk to an adult and get them to clear this up with me.'

A glitch

'I'm a little worried but I can handle this one on my own.'

2 3 4

1   5

A disaster or tragedy

'This worry is scaring me. I can't stop thinking about it. I need to talk to an adult and work out a plan – fast.'

Dealing with Disappointment

Explanation

Disappointment has to be one of the trickiest feelings to deal with. There are so many different disappointments to experience, and the intensity depends on what is at stake and what other feelings become entangled at the time. As an example a child may feel mildly disappointed because they scored poorly on a piece of work at school. Suddenly, their disappointment soars to a whole new level through embarrassment as classmates discover just how poor their score was.

All things considered, most children deal with day-to-day disappointments reasonably well, but the children who are our focus tend to struggle with faster feelings that are often on display for all to see. Although the term 'social and emotional delay' helps to explain their challenge, most also carry a common legacy. They perceive that they have experienced more disappointment than most others. They are quick to mention disappointing experiences: last in the race, last to learn a new skill, last to be picked for a team and consistently overlooked to be invited to birthday parties. Experiencing more disappointment, more often than most, actually heightens their sensitivity to it. It erodes their self-esteem and raises frustration. Disappointment is so often at the core of many anger difficulties.

To be honest, the skills required to deal effectively with disappointment take some time to be learned. Most of us have battled for years to master the art of looking calm, confident and resilient despite feeling upset and disappointed.

The purpose of this lesson is to explain to students the following essential facts about why they encounter disappointment and how they can best deal with it:

1 *Disappointment is unavoidable. Everyone experiences it.*

2 *Disappointment happens when things do not go our way, or to plan.*

3 *We can be disappointed in ourselves, disappointed in another, disappointed for another or disappointed about a situation.*

4 *The best way to deal with disappointment is to use positive thinking. When we think positively we give ourselves the best chance to find a sensible way to manage it.*

Materials required for Lesson 12

- Whiteboard/butcher's paper and a marker

- Post *What's the Buzz?* group rules (located on p. 20; alternatively, they can be downloaded from www.whatsthebuzz.net.au)

- Place an outline of the lesson on the whiteboard/butcher's paper

- A ten pin bowling set with a ball

- Ten small paper bags – write messages on each paper bag (see *Show me the Buzz* for messages)

- One bag of small sweets (jellybeans . . . or similar)

- One roll of sellotape

- Photocopy One 'Disappointment, my catastrophe scale', for each student (located in the photocopiable resources at the end of this lesson; alternatively, they can be downloaded from www.whatsthebuzz.net.au)

- 1 medium sized ball and one bowling pin (reuse items from the ten pin bowling set mentioned above) for the game 'Guard the Pin'

- 4 sheets of large format graph paper and pencils to share for the game 'Boxes'

- Organise the gold nuggets, cubes to build a friendship wall, group rule and reminder cards or a similar feedback device (see the chapter, Practical Considerations)

- Organise a small gift or a reward token for each child

- Prepare handouts for parent(s):

  – One copy of this lesson for each parent to read

  – One copy of *After the Buzz: social thinking ideas for parents* for each parent to read (section follows this lesson).

Lesson 12

Arrange participants into a social circle. Welcome them. Draw everyone's attention to the group rules. Display the feedback device to encourage positive social behaviours (see section on feedback ideas in the chapter, Practical Considerations). Explain that if successful each student may leave with a small gift.

1. What's the Buzz?

What's the Buzz? introduces students to this lesson's topic and the new set of skills to be learned. Explain that today we're talking about disappointment, and it's one of the trickiest feelings to deal with. Begin by saying to the group:

Do you know that disappointment is unavoidable?

It happens to everyone.

It happens when things don't work out the way you had planned or hoped.

You can be disappointed in yourself, disappointed in another, disappointed for someone, or disappointed about a situation

Tell me the things that have made you feel disappointed. Record them on the whiteboard/butcher's paper. Typical responses include:

- losing a game

- being the worst at something

- being last

- feeling embarrassed

- not getting what you wanted

- missing out

- being rejected by others

- dealing with a broken promise

- being overlooked

- having plans changed or cancelled

- When you have to stop doing something you're enjoying

- being told 'no'.

Do you know the best way to deal with it?

Use *positive thinking* because it stops disappointment from erupting into angry behaviours you will later regret.

How to use *positive thinking* to deal with disappointment:

1 If you can, move away from the person or whatever has made you disappointed.

2 Tell yourself exactly what the disappointment is. For example, 'I feel disappointed because I missed out.'

3 Remind yourself how big the disappointment should be. In other words, rate it on a catastrophe scale just as we used for measuring how serious a worry should be (introduce the 'Disappointment, my catastrophe scale' to students).

4 Take a deep breath and put a *positive thought* into your mind:

   – 'I can handle it.'

   – 'That's life! I'll be okay.'

   – 'Worse things could happen. Let's find a good side to this.'

   – 'It probably won't matter tomorrow.'

   – 'I'll just go with it. This feeling won't last.'

   – 'This isn't what I wanted, but I can handle it.'

Lastly, do something that helps to carry the *positive thought*. This is the time to use one of your favourite 'calm-down' ideas you developed in Lesson 9.

(Write 'How to use *positive thinking* to deal with disappointment' on the whiteboard or butcher's paper)

2. Show me the Buzz

Show me the Buzz gives students the opportunity to practise and show they understand the new skill set. Explain this game involves practising how to cope with disappointment!

Bring out the ten pin bowling set, or similar. Arrange the pins and tape a small paper bag on each pin. Each paper bag has one of the messages below written on it and each bag contains two treats (we use jellybeans).

Messages recorded on each paper bag

• Eat us.

• Eat one and give the other away.

• Give us away to someone else.

• Don't touch us!

- Don't eat me now. Save me for after.

- Sorry, you cannot eat us.

- Choose someone taller than you to have these.

- Choose two others to share these.

- These are for the facilitator!

Participants take turns to bowl the ball and knock a pin down. If successful, they read the instruction on the paper bag and must follow it. This game is great fun, but be alert because some will struggle with their disappointment! Reinforce *positive thinking*, playing to have fun and how serious the disappointment should rate on the catastrophe scale.

3. Do you know the Buzz?

Do you know the Buzz? is a fast-moving question time. Its purpose is to consolidate the concepts gathered in the lesson. Arrange the group into a social circle and hand participants the 'Disappointment, my catastrophe scale' you showed them earlier in the lesson. Ask each student to rate one of the disappointments below on the catastrophe scale and offer a *positive thought* to deal with it. Encourage everyone to have a go. Keep it quick!

Round 1

Disappointing scenarios

- Your video game controller won't work and you badly wanted to play your new game.

- You have lost a valuable old coin that is very special to you and your family.

- Everyone else has been invited to go to a birthday party, but you haven't.

- You are not with any of your friends in your new class.

- Someone ate all the chocolate and you missed out.

- You miss out on going to the movies because your Mum feels sick.

- Your friends are picking groups and you are the last to be picked.

- Dad promised to bring a special treat home with him. He completely forgot.

- You are waiting for your friend to come over. Just as he should be arriving he phones and says he can't come.

- The football team you play for keeps on losing. It's embarrassing!

- Every time you try to kick a goal you miss!

- Your mother and father hand you your birthday present. It is not what you wanted.

4. The Buzz

During *The Buzz* students play games that help them to practise their newly learned skills.

Guard the Pin (exciting for all ages)

This game requires one ball and one pin. The ball and a pin from the ten pin bowling set used earlier are ideal. Arrange players to stand in a large circle facing into the centre. A pin is placed in the centre of the circle and a guard is chosen to protect it. The guard stands in the centre of the circle near the pin. The aim of the game is for the players in the circle to knock down the pin with the ball by bowling it over. All throws must be underarm bowls. The person who eventually knocks down the pin is able to become the new guard. Players quickly learn that unless they cooperate and communicate by rolling the ball to one another it is very difficult to get the ball past the guard.

Statues (exciting for all ages)

On 'go' ask players to run about a designated space. After a few moments call out, 'Statues!' All players are expected to freeze, and just for the record, they may continue to breathe and blink. Players will freeze in all sorts of tortuous positions. Your task is to walk up to each of them, and without touching them, see if you can do or say something that will cause them to lose concentration and giggle or move. This is a lot of fun and players adore playing it over and over. You may wish to vary the game by removing players from the game as they are caught or making a player 'it' when they are caught moving.

20 Questions, or Fewer (passive for all ages)

Think of something. To illustrate this let's say you think of a carrot. The group has 20 questions to guess that you are thinking of a carrot. The first player might say, 'What category is it? Animal, vegetable or mineral?' In this case you would answer, 'Vegetable!' The next student might say, 'Does it grow on a tree?' And so the game continues until a participant guesses it is a carrot. The player who guesses begins the next round.

5. Goodbye Buzz

Bid students a warm goodbye and remind them to take their folders, which contain:

- a copy of this lesson for parents

- a copy of *After the Buzz: social thinking ideas for parents*

- a spare copy of 'Disappointment, my catastrophe scale'.

As feedback for thoughtful behaviours each student may leave with a small gift.

After the Buzz: social thinking ideas for parents

Lesson 12: Dealing with Disappointment

This lesson examined the facts about disappointment. In summary, they are:

1 Disappointment is unavoidable.

2 Disappointment happens to each of us when things do not go to plan.

3 We can be disappointed in ourselves, disappointed in another, disappointed for another or disappointed about a situation.

4 The best way to deal with disappointment is to use *positive thinking*. When we think positively we give ourselves the best chance to constructively navigate around the disappointment.

To be honest, the skills required to deal successfully with disappointment take time to learn. Most of us have battled for years to master the art of looking calm, confident and resilient despite feeling upset or disappointed. In the meantime here are a few ideas to improve your child's ability to deal with disappointment and to help you guide them in positive directions.

• Coping with disappointment

   Naturally, most parents have an urge to protect their children from disappointment. Yet, a child's ability to cope with it is built through learning how to deal with it. Disappointment is essential for healthy emotional growth. It is through the pains of childhood, with balanced parental input, that children are prepared to deal with more complex disappointments later in life. Keep this in mind and refrain from rushing in and fixing their problem or refusing to let them feel disappointed. Instead, help them work through their disappointed feelings by acknowledging what they are feeling and by offering wise levels of support.

• Put the disappointment into words

   Encourage children to put disappointment into words. Ask, 'Are you crying because you're disappointed about being too sick to go to Shane's party?' Try to acknowledge your child's feelings, but also focus on creating a positive way forward.

- Plan ahead

  In situations where disappointment is likely, be sure to plan ahead! Discuss the upcoming event and pinpoint the moments that are likely to cause disappointment. Offer a compensatory action to support your child. One way may be to hold their hand at a critical moment so they are reminded that you care, the moment will pass and all will be well. Spending time discussing what is likely to happen helps children to find extra emotional resources later on when it counts.

- Disappointments at school

  'Break cards' work for students of all ages at school. The idea is that a card may sit on the teacher's desk or in the student's pocket. At times when frustration or disappointment threatens the student uses the card. They hand it to the teacher and move to a pre-assigned area or to a predetermined 'safe person' away from the classroom to have time to calm down. The rules are developed by the student and teacher, and are detailed on the cards themselves. Being given permission to walk away releases the child from the pressure of immediate reform, which of course can push distressed students right over the edge. In this way they have a chance to regain poise and regroup their emotions.

- Identify your child's 'islands of competence'

  Loretta Giorcelli's (2000) work reminds us how important it is to highlight and maximise the areas our children feel successful and confident about. Involve your children (and yourself) in activities, clubs and associations where they can develop their talents and interests. This is a good way to support the growth of esteem and confidence within a social context. Without this, it is too easy for children to interpret disappointment as yet another failure.

- Teach protective strategies

  Show your child how to give a quick humorous response to a disappointing or frustrating situation. A casual remark can go a long way to help a potential victim look as though they are dealing with disappointment. However, most children need training and re-training on how to do this. Above all else, teach your children not to immediately look crest-fallen when disappointing situations arise.

- A disappointment shield

  This is a powerful helper for children who enjoy visualising. Ask them to sketch a picture of themselves on to paper. Next, suggest they draw a force field or a shield as protection. Teach them when and how to charge the shield up so disappointment does not reach their sensitive heart. Draw the shield powered up with words and phrases they usually find hurtful and disappointing simply bouncing off and disappearing into thin air. A disappointment shield may not be totally impenetrable, but it can certainly help your child to buy time while in public. With practice, this can become a very powerful defense.

After the Buzz ... Lesson 12

- Discuss the worksheet, 'Disappointment, my catastrophe scale' with your child

  This is intended to be a visual helper to assess the intensity of a disappointment. By rating a disappointment children are assisted to put it into perspective. It helps them consider, 'How big is this disappointment?' 'Will it really matter tomorrow?' 'Is it better to let it go so I don't spoil the rest of the day?' It may be a useful device to use in the future at home.

  Another idea is to write a humorous story about a time when you were disappointed and handled it badly (a little fictitious licence can make it entertaining). Sometimes it is therapeutic for children to learn that their mothers and fathers also struggled with this tricky feeling when they were younger.

The final word on dealing with disappointment is to be understanding. Not all children bounce back from it at the same rate. What is important is that your response helps them to prepare to cope as best they can for the unavoidable disappointments that will surely crop up in the future.

Photocopiable resources now follow, and don't forget the online resources at www.whatsthebuzz.net.au!

After the Buzz . . . Lesson 12

What's the Buzz?

Disappointment, my catastrophe scale

Name: _____

Think: how serious is this disappointment?

Train yourself to use this scale and rate your disappointment.

By rating it, the disappointment stays as real as it should be, and you can find a solution.

'He hates not being a winner every time.'

MY DISAPPOINTMENT SCALE

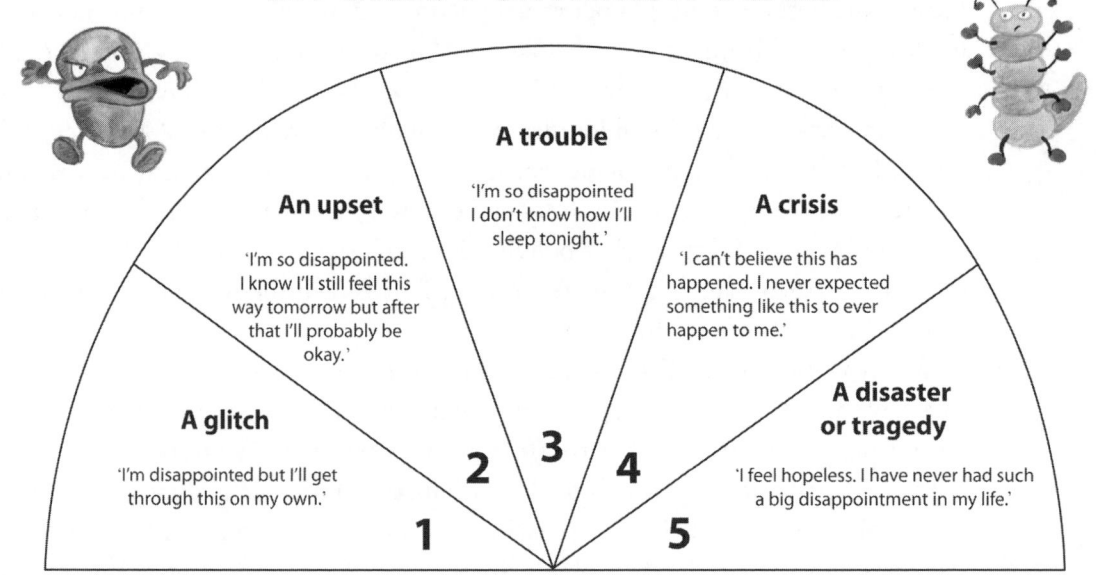

An upset
'I'm so disappointed. I know I'll still feel this way tomorrow but after that I'll probably be okay.'

A trouble
'I'm so disappointed I don't know how I'll sleep tonight.'

A crisis
'I can't believe this has happened. I never expected something like this to ever happen to me.'

A glitch
'I'm disappointed but I'll get through this on my own.'

A disaster or tragedy
'I feel hopeless. I have never had such a big disappointment in my life.'

1   2   3   4   5

Responding to Bullying

Explanation

Social studies researchers continue to collect data about bullying. From it we learn that no kindergarten, school or college is free from bullying and no student is safe from it. We know that about 17 per cent of students are bullied in most primary schools each week, and by and large this takes place outside of the classroom (Rigby, 2002a). The act of bullying is defined as repeated physical harm, intimidation, purposeful isolation, name calling, systematic 'put-downs', spreading of hurtful lies and teasing, frightening text messages or attacks via MSN (Rigby, 2002b). The general profile of a bully is impossible to describe. A few bullies are manipulative thugs, but most swing between being an occasional victim to using bully behaviours themselves to deal with problematic social situations. An Australia-wide study conducted by Western Australia's Edith Cowan University and the Flinders University of South Australia surveyed 7,000 children from 124 schools (Cross, *et al.* 2009; Slee, *et al.* 2008). It revealed that the incidence of bullying rises to 23 per cent by year nine and that recipients and perpetrators are evenly split. Many of the young people surveyed commented that cyber bullying is on the rise and is hard to deal with, but refuse to tell their parents as they fear they will have their mobile phones taken away or may be banned from the computer.

We have also learned that absenteeism is greater among the bullied, and so too is social withdrawal, anxiety, depression, declines in academic performance, suicidal thoughts and attempts at self-harm (Rigby and Slee, 1999). As a response to counter bullying behaviours we have seen a lot of initiatives implemented in schools. While the media is always quick to popularise such programmes they have yielded only average improvements. In fact, about 40 per cent of students say it is better to put up with bullying than to tell (Cross, *et al.* 2009). They say telling makes things worse. Once they tell an adult they face the unpredictable reaction from the bully, risk other students becoming involved and feel as though their powerlessness deepens. Students repeatedly say that most teachers and parents do not appreciate the depth of bullying, and when they do, they haven't the time to guide and support the recovery of those involved. In sharing this, our children offer us a monumental challenge.

Without the development of a culture focused on improving ways to communicate and reconcile differences, traditional school anti-bullying programmes can only ever deliver mediocre results.

The objective of this lesson is to alert students to what bullying is. This is critical because students who are bullied over a longer period are more often those who struggle with social thinking and social skills. Quite a few are not sure how to recognise a bully, and when they do, they respond in a way that gives the bully satisfying feedback. Similarly, quite a few find themselves being accused of bully behaviour because they cannot get their own way or express feelings aptly.

Materials required for Lesson 13

- Whiteboard/butcher's paper and a marker

- Post *What's the Buzz?* group rules (located on p. 20; alternatively, they can be downloaded from www.whatsthebuzz.net.au)

- Place an outline of the lesson on the whiteboard/butcher's paper

- Prepare the 'Guide sheet: how to deal with bullying for each student (located in the photocopiable resources at the end of this lesson; alternatively, they can be downloaded from www.whatsthebuzz.net.au

- Prepare 'Possible bullying solution' cards for *Show me the Buzz?* activity (located in the photocopiable resources at the end of this lesson; alternatively, they can be downloaded from www.whatsthebuzz.net.au)

- One roll of masking tape for the activity 'Possible bullying solutions' and the game 'Lonely Little Ghost'

- Eight sheets of white A3 paper for the game 'Draw Me If You Can?'

- Purchase an inexpensive bubble blowing kit for each student

- Eight pencils and coloured markers

- Organise the gold nuggets, cubes to build a friendship wall, group rule and reminder cards or a similar feedback device (see the chapter, Practical Considerations)

- Organise a small gift or a reward token for each child

- Prepare handouts for parent(s):

  - One copy of this lesson for each parent to read

  - One copy of *After the Buzz: social thinking ideas for parents* for each parent to read (section follows this lesson).

Lesson 13

Arrange participants into a social circle. Welcome them.

Draw everyone's attention to the group rules. Display the feedback device to encourage positive social behaviours (see section on feedback ideas in the chapter, Practical Considerations). Explain that if successful each student may leave with a small gift.

1. What's the Buzz?

What's the Buzz? introduces students to this lesson's topic and the new set of skills to be learned. Ask participants what bullying is. To gauge their depth of understanding add the following to the discussion: name calling, repeated laughing and making fun of someone, spreading lies, aggression, ganging up, ignoring without any reason, mean or aggressive text messaging, MSN attacks.

Definition of bullying behaviour

> Bullying = desire to hurt + hurtful action + power imbalance + repetition + unjust use of power + evident enjoyment by aggressor + sense of being oppressed by the victim.

> (Rigby, 2004)

(Write this on the whiteboard or butcher's paper)

Allow students to discuss this definition. It tells us that bullying is serious. Ask if any of them have ever been bullied, and how it felt.

Role-plays

The way we respond to someone bullying makes a big difference.

Ask students to watch the three role-plays and work out whether the victim is responding in a way where the bully feels rewarded or disappointed.

Role-play 1: rewarding a bully

> Student volunteer (aggressive tone of voice, wanting to be hurtful):
> *'I saw you at basketball training last night. What was the coach thinking when he picked you? You're hopeless. I've been talking to everyone about you and they agree with me.'*

> Facilitator (arms folded, head down, taking a weak, sulky, intimidated stance):
> *'Be quiet. You're weak too. What would you know?'*

Invite feedback: 'did the victim's response reward or disappoint the bully?'

Role-play 2: rewarding a bully

Student volunteer (aggressive tone of voice, wanting to be hurtful):
'I saw you at basketball training last night. What was the coach thinking when he picked you? You're such a klutz. I've been talking to everyone about you and they agree with me.'

Facilitator (pushing, shoving and shouting at the bully while defending him/herself):
'I hate you, loser. I hate your stupid friends too. You can all get lost' (storms off kicking the ground).

Invite feedback: 'Did the victim's response reward or disappoint the bully?'

Role-play 3: disappointing a bully

Student volunteer (aggressive tone of voice, wanting to be hurtful):
'I saw you at basketball training last night. What was the coach thinking when he picked you? You're hopeless. I've been talking to everyone about you and they agree with me.'

Facilitator (looking calm and composed as if the bully's nasty words don't matter):
'So what' (shrugs shoulders). 'That's your opinion' (rolls eyes and walks away).

Invite feedback: 'Did the victim's response reward or disappoint the bully?'

Review: 'What have we learned from these three role-plays?'

Mention that occasionally giving non-rewarding behaviours to a bully may make them angry. This is the time to seek help from friends, teachers, the Principal and your parents.

Also point out that you will include a guide sheet on how to deal with bullying in their folder that they can share with their parents. Hold it up so students can see it.

2. Show me the Buzz

Show me the Buzz gives students the opportunity to practise and show they understand the new skill set.

Arrange the students into a large social circle. Place all of the 'Possible bullying solution' cards on the floor face down in the middle. Provide each participant with a marker or pencil. Ask group members to select one card each, write their name on it and read it.

Explain that the cards show a way to solve bullying problems in either a HELPFUL or UNHELPFUL way. Their task is to fasten the card to the whiteboard or butcher's paper in the column headed HELPFUL SOLUTIONS if they think the statement is helpful, and in the column headed UNHELPFUL SOLUTIONS if they believe the solution will not be HELPFUL. Once the group has finished posting the cards, move around the circle and ask each participant why they made their choice. This will stimulate some interesting discussion.

Possible bullying solutions

- If you think someone has done something to bully you . . .
  Look them in the eye and say, 'That's just what you think. It doesn't make you right.'

- If you think someone has done something to bully you . . .
  Say, 'thanks', shrug your shoulders and walk away.

- If you think someone has done something to bully you . . .
  Say nothing and go on with what you are doing.

- If you think someone has done something to bully you . . .
  Shrug your shoulders and say, 'You'd have no idea you big fat loser!'

- If you think someone has done something to bully you . . .
  Laugh and say, 'Good one! But not today thanks!'

- If you think someone has done something to bully you . . .
  Yawn and say, 'Sorry, what did you say?'

- If you think someone has done something to bully you . . .
  Scream at them.

- If you think someone has done something to bully you . . .
  Kick them and run away.

- If you think someone has done something to bully you . . .
  Run and tell a teacher.

- If you think someone has done something to bully you . . .
  Spread mean lies about them.

- If you think someone has done something to bully you . . .
  Say, 'I don't like you being nasty to me! It hurts my feelings!'

- If you think someone has done something to bully you . . .
  Look them in the eye and say, 'You should go now or I'll go to the Principal.'

- If you think someone has done something to bully you . . .
  Say, 'I don't know what you've got against me because I think you're okay.'

- If you think someone has done something to bully you . . .
  Say, 'We should talk about this later' (and walk away).

- If you think someone has done something to bully you . . .
  Wiggle your hips and do a funny dance. Then say, 'Sticks and stones might break my bones, but you're words are funny!'

- If you think someone has done something to bully you . . .
  Send them a mean text message to teach them a lesson.

- If you think someone has done something to bully you . . .
  Go home and talk about it with Mum or Dad.

- If you think someone has done something to bully you . . .
  Go home and make Mum and Dad fix it.

- If you think someone has done something to bully you . . .
  Stare at them. Move closer to them. Say nothing.

- If you think someone has done something to bully you . . .
  Twirl around three times, make a squawking sound and run away flapping your arms.

- If you think someone has done something to bully you . . .
  Take out a note pad and pencil. Tell them you will write down what they say so you can share it with your teacher and principal.

3. Do you know the Buzz?

Do you know the Buzz? is a fast-moving question time. Its purpose is to consolidate the concepts gathered in the lesson. Encourage everyone to have a go. Here is the challenge.

Decide which statements are true, false or confusing. Put your thumbs up if you think the statement is true, thumbs down if you think the statement is false and put your thumbs to the side if you think the statement should be challenged.

Round 1

- Bullies want to control others.
- Some kids bully because they think it makes them popular.
- Some kids bully because they think it makes them look tough.
- How you react to a bully will make them bully you more or less.
- Always get angry at the bully because it scares them away.
- Cry because the bully will feel sorry for you and stop.
- Get friends to gang up on them and teach them a lesson.
- Never look a bully in the eye.
- Some kids use bully behaviours because they can't get their way.
- A good idea is to try to treat the bully gently.
- When you get bullied run away saying you'll tell on them and you hate them.
- If you think you are being bullied you should be talking to your teacher.
- Bullies use other people, text messaging and computers to bully.
- Everyone bullies sometimes. It's just what happens.

4. The Buzz

During *The Buzz* students play games that help them to practise their newly learned skills. The theme for the first game is of course based around teasing, but has an enjoyable twist to it.

Lonely Little Ghost (exciting for all ages)

To begin, a Lonely Little Ghost who wants some friends needs to be chosen. The Lonely Little Ghost wants to make new ghost friends, but the friends are not very nice at all!

The Lonely Little Ghost sits on a chair in the haunted house. Use masking tape on the floor (about 3 metres by 3 metres) to make a square that represents the haunted house. Players (little ghost friends) get to tease the ghost with silly faces, ridiculous walking and mindless comments – but there's a catch! They can only tease as they walk about inside the haunted house. As they do this the Lonely Little Ghost can jump up and try to tag one of the teasing little ghosts before they get away.

If tagged within the haunted house this player adds a chair and joins the Lonely Little Ghost as another Lonely Little Ghost. The game continues until a nominated number of players are caught (usually four). The idea is never to be caught!

As the game finishes ask students to describe the difference in feelings between being a Lonely Little Ghost and a teaser.

Draw Me if You Can? (passive for older students)

Divide the group into pairs. One player becomes the 'communicator' and the other the 'drawer'. Provide the 'drawer' from each pair with a white A3 sheet of paper as well as plenty of pencils and coloured markers. Ask these students to withdraw to a private space in the room.

Gather the 'communicators' in close and show them a simple line drawing you have drawn on a white A3 sheet of paper. It may be as basic as a circle divided into quarters, but with each quarter separated from the other using different colours. Older students revel in the process of having to remember a more complex design.

Once the 'communicators' have seen the drawing they return to their partner. Their task is to get their partner (the drawer) to draw, as accurately as they can, what they saw. All the 'communicator' can do to make this happen is talk the drawer through the process. Once each pair have finished ask all players to return to the social circle to compare their attempt with yours. If time permits, get 'communicators' and 'drawers' to swap roles and try a new drawing together.

Blowing Bubbles (exciting for all ages)

This quiet, therapeutic activity can be played inside or outside. Purchase an inexpensive bubble blowing kit for each student and sit them tightly together in the social circle. The goal is for players to face the centre of the circle and make sure none of the bubbles land on players or inside the circle. Feel free to expand the size of the circle!

5. Goodbye Buzz

Bid students a warm goodbye and remind them to take their folders, which contain:

- a copy of this lesson for parents

- a copy of *After the Buzz: social thinking ideas for parents*

- a copy of the 'Guide sheet: how to deal with bully behaviours'.

As feedback for thoughtful behaviours each student may leave with a small gift.

After the Buzz: social thinking ideas for parents

Lesson 13: Responding to Bullying

This lesson alerted your child to aspects about bullying; how to recognise a bully and bullying behaviours, and how to respond skilfully without giving the bully satisfying feedback. It is not possible to isolate your child from bullying encounters, but it is possible to take a few steps to sharpen their awareness and responses to this damaging behaviour.

*   *Bullying =*

    'desire to hurt + hurtful action + power imbalance + repetition + unjust use of power + evident enjoyment by aggressor + sense of being oppressed by the victim' (Rigby, 2004).

    Teach your child the difference between bullying, being treated unfairly and not being able to get their own way. There are worlds of difference!

*   The role of the bystander in bullying

    A new understanding about responses to bullying behaviours has emerged. It is no longer acceptable for anyone to stand by and witness someone being bullied without doing something about it. Everyone in the school and local community has an obligation to intervene in a way that keeps them safe.

*   Prepare for it

    A casual response to a bully can go a long way to help a victim look as though they are resilient. Bullies often target a characteristic they think will be another's weakness. Alert your child to the fact that how they respond will either deflect the behaviour or encourage it. Many children need continuous coaching to carry this off with poise:

    The quick answer
    Help them rehearse two or three quick replies so that when they are 'put down' they might roll their eyes and say, 'Yeah, you'd be right' or 'None of your beeswax' or 'Whatever' or 'Takes one to know one' and walk away.

    Dog poo on the shoe
    As somebody draws close to your child and is committed to annoy or tease them they need to twitch their nose a little and look hard at the teaser's feet. Help them to rehearse saying, 'Oh, something stinks. You've got dog poo on your shoe!' Then walk away.

The teasing shield

This can be a powerful skin-thickener for children with strong imaginations. Help them to practise surrounding themselves with an imaginary tease-proof shield. The shield cannot be penetrated by hurtful words; they just bounce back at the bully. Teach them how to power it up with their knowledge that bullying is wrong and bullies actually need helping. Help them to practise maintaining a relaxed, smiling face as you deliver a barrage of mean words. With practice, this can become a very powerful defense.

The smart advantage!

As raised previously, the act of staying calm gives our brains the best chance to make the best choices. Teach your child that when someone says something hurtful or threatening they have choices to deal with the problem: smile, shrug, walk away, tell a joke, ignore, run, roll your eyes, duck for cover, flap your wings, be quiet or say you agree. Teach them to press the 'delete key' in their mind or to shrink those they are having trouble with into little babies with smelly nappies. In this way they can say, 'It just doesn't matter', and it really doesn't.

Caution: these ideas are not concerned with the exchange of insults. Exchanging insults will be to your child's disadvantage. They are offered as an offhand way to give an unexpected response, recover a little control and disengage.

- Talk about bullying

Conversation about bullies and bullying sends a signal to all children that 'bully psychology' is understood. Books such as *Queen Bees and Wannabes* by Rosalind Wiseman and films such as *Mean Girls* have contributed to our understandings by popularising the psychology behind bullying. Let your children know they can talk to you, teachers, friends at school, friends outside school, other trusted parents, a relative or a caregiver. Talking about it is healthy. It is not the same as 'telling tales'.

- Listen

Avoid rushing in, trying to fix the problem or blaming someone. As you listen the opportunity to understand the situation presents itself, and as your child talks they are better able to grasp what has taken place. It also gives them a chance to generate ideas to repair the situation.

- Bullying is WRONG

All children have a right to feel safe at school and at home. All schools have bullying policies. Let your child know this. There are a number of excellent websites for adults and children to learn how to cope with bullying:

Mainly for children:

- www.bullyingnoway.com.au
- www.caper.com.au
- www.headroom.net.au/cubby/index.html
- www.kids.novita.org.au

After the Buzz … Lesson 13

Mainly for parents:

- www.antibullying.net/
- www.cyh.com
- www.healthinsite.gov.au/topics/Bullying
- www.kids.nsw.gov.au/exchange/9/bullying.html
- www.lfcc.on.ca/bully.htm
- www.42explore2.com/bully.htm

- What to do when bullying happens

All schools take bullying seriously. Usually, a written plan is developed to help everyone recover and learn. A plan often follows this layout:

First, the nature and severity of the difficulty is clarified.

Decisions are made about how the victim and bully can be best supported. The victim's spirits may be buoyed by assisting them to develop a network of sensitive peer confidants. The bully may need support to learn how to interact in more acceptable ways. And, if other students have been involved, a set of procedures are created so that they know what to do to recover the situation.

A determination is made to see if the victim could safely participate with the bully in a process of restoration. This is an ideal way to move forward.

The victim is kept informed about what is happening. Frequently, schools respond suitably to bullying, but the victim is left out of the information loop. They then feel powerless and believe nothing has happened to rectify the situation.

Methods to monitor the interactions of both students, especially at break times, are arranged. By doing this progress can be measured.

Opportunities are developed for both students to 'check in' with a teacher or counsellor to help monitor progress.

Sometimes help is required in the form of social skills training or assertiveness training programmes. The victim may need to develop 'fitting in' skills and the bully may need to learn how to use their need to control in a more pro-social way.

A time is made to meet, review and decide on whether the strategies put in place are helping. If the bullying problem continues, despite committed and thoughtful interventions, it is sensible to consider a change of class, or perhaps a change of school. The evidence suggests that most students who have suffered bullying are not bullied in new situations (Rigby, 2002a).

- 'Guide sheet: how to deal with bullying'

You will notice this handout in your child's folder. Not only is it useful to base a conversation around, but it is something that can be used to refer back to in the future.

Photocopiable resources now follow, and don't forget the online resources at www.whatsthebuzz.net.au!

What's the Buzz?

Guide sheet: how to deal with bullying

How do you know if you are being bullied?

Bullying = desire to hurt + hurtful action + power imbalance + repetition + unjust use of power + evident enjoyment by aggressor + sense of being oppressed by the victim (Rigby, 2004).

What to do

1   Make sure your behaviour does not reward the bully. Respond in a way that disappoints them.

2   Always look and sound confident

How to look

-   stand tall, give eye contact and look relaxed

-   if you must respond do it calmly

-   keep yourself safe and use one or some of these:

    ignore   walk away   smile   laugh

    yawn   roll your eyes   shrug your shoulders

What to say

-   keep your voice light and smooth:

    'Not this again. . .'   'Haven't you got anything better to do?'

    'This is getting boring'   'I'm sorry you do this because I think you're okay.'

    'Thanks for the advice.'

3   Stay close to safe places and safe people (close to the yard duty teacher, the staff room, other dependable friends)

4   Talk to Mum, Dad, teacher, principal and friends about what's happening. It helps to talk because they will have good advice and can keep an eye on you. They can help if you want them to.

What's the Buzz?

Possible bullying solution cards

What's the Buzz? Possible bullying solution card 1

 If you think someone has done something to bully you …

Look them in the eye and say, 'That's just what you think. It doesn't make you right.'

What's the Buzz? Possible bullying solution card 2

 If you think someone has done something to bully you …

Say, 'thanks', shrug your shoulders and walk away.

What's the Buzz? Possible bullying solution card 3

 If you think someone has done something to bully you …

Say nothing and go on with what you are doing.

What's the Buzz? Possible bullying solution card 4

 If you think someone has done something to bully you …

Shrug your shoulders and say, 'You'd have no idea you big fat loser!'

What's the Buzz? Possible bullying solution card 5

 If you think someone has done something to bully you …

Laugh and say, 'Good one! But not today thanks!'

What's the Buzz? Possible bullying solution card 6

If you think someone has done something to bully you …

Yawn and say, 'Sorry, what did you say?'

What's the Buzz?

Possible bullying solution cards

continued . . .

What's the Buzz? Possible bullying solution	card 7

 If you think someone has done something to bully you …

Scream at them.

What's the Buzz? Possible bullying solution	card 8

 If you think someone has done something to bully you …

Kick them and run away.

What's the Buzz? Possible bullying solution	card 9

 If you think someone has done something to bully you …

Run and tell a teacher.

What's the Buzz? Possible bullying solution	card 10

 If you think someone has done something to bully you …

Spread mean lies about them.

What's the Buzz? Possible bullying solution	card 11

 If you think someone has done something to bully you …

Say, 'I don't like you being nasty to me! It hurts my feelings!'

What's the Buzz? Possible bullying solution	card 12

If you think someone has done something to bully you …

Look them in the eye and say, 'You should go now or I'll go to the Principal.'

What's the Buzz?

Possible bullying solution cards

continued . . .

What's the Buzz?   Possible bullying solution   card 13

If you think someone has done something to bully you …

Say, 'I don't know what you've got against me because I think you're okay.'

What's the Buzz?   Possible bullying solution   card 14

If you think someone has done something to bully you …

Say, 'We should talk about this later' (and walk away).

What's the Buzz?   Possible bullying solution   card 15

If you think someone has done something to bully you …

Wiggle your hips and do a funny dance. Then say, 'Sticks and stones might break my bones, but your words are funny!'

What's the Buzz?   Possible bullying solution   card 16

If you think someone has done something to bully you …

Send them a mean text message to teach them a lesson.

What's the Buzz?   Possible bullying solution   card 17

If you think someone has done something to bully you …

Go home and talk about it with Mum or Dad.

What's the Buzz?

Possible bullying solution cards

continued . . .

What's the Buzz?   Possible bullying solution   card 18

If you think someone has done something to bully you …

Go home and make Mum and Dad fix it.

What's the Buzz?   Possible bullying solution   card 19

If you think someone has done something to bully you …

Stare at them. Move closer to them. Say nothing.

What's the Buzz?   Possible bullying solution   card 20

If you think someone has done something to bully you …

Twirl around three times, make a squawking sound and run away flapping your arms.

What's the Buzz?   Possible bullying solution   card 21

If you think someone has done something to bully you …

Take out a note pad and pencil. Tell them you will write down what they say so you can share it with your teacher and principal.

The Connecting Art of Conversation

Explanation

Developing conversational skills is an investment in getting along with others. However, developing the ability to pitch it in the right way and at the right time does not come easily for everyone. Some are able to freely create natural and engaging conversations while others are just not sure what to say, how to say it or whether what they have to say will interest others.

This lesson contains the essential tips to develop conversational skills. It looks at the rules associated with conversation and highlights practical steps to make improvements. It also aims to reassure participants that conversational skills may look easy, but the truth is a good conversationalist relies on using a series of small, intricate skills. These include looking and listening, reading body language, judging interest, timing, physical proximity, appropriate topic selection, conversation connecting abilities, compromise, assertiveness and confidence. With so many skills linked to quality conversation, it is not surprising that for those already wrestling with one developmental issue or another, the art of conversation will take longer to master.

As conversational skills are grasped, and confidence grows, others are likely to respond positively as they sense this connecting skill in action.

Materials required for Lesson 14

- Whiteboard/butcher's paper and a marker

- Post *What's the Buzz?* group rules (located on p. 20; alternatively, they can be downloaded from www.whatsthebuzz.net.au)

- Place an outline of the lesson on the whiteboard/butcher's paper

- Prepare one set of 'conversational connectors' for each participant (located in the photocopiable resources at the end of this lesson; alternatively, they can be downloaded from www.whatsthebuzz.net.au)

- One stop watch, or similar

- Organise the gold nuggets, cubes to build a friendship wall, group rule and reminder cards or a similar feedback device (see the chapter, Practical Considerations)

- Organise a small gift or a reward token for each child

- Prepare handouts for parent(s):

  - One copy of this lesson for each parent to read

  - One copy of *After the Buzz: social thinking ideas for parents* for each parent to read (section follows this lesson).

Lesson 14

Arrange participants into a social circle. Welcome them. Draw everyone's attention to the group rules. Display the feedback device to encourage positive social behaviours (see section on feedback ideas in the chapter, Practical Considerations). Explain that if successful each student may leave with a small gift.

1. What's the Buzz?

What's the Buzz? introduces students to this lesson's topic and the new set of skills to be learned.

Begin by suddenly speaking to a co-facilitator or student volunteer using a loud, excited voice. Say, 'Hey, I've been meaning to talk to you'.

'I wanted to talk to you as well', the volunteer will reply (this short skit needs to be rehearsed without the knowledge of other participants).

Then, for the next thirty seconds talk directly at one another. What the group will witness is an overwhelming display of parallel monologues; not a conversation at all.

Once finished turn to the group and say, 'today's lesson is about how to have successful conversations, but I've got a feeling that conversation didn't go so well. What went wrong?'

Encourage group members to offer their opinions.

Briefly explain the steps to make conversations sparkle.

How to make a conversation sparkle

Before you start, look about and think: is this a good time to start this conversation with this person?

1 Begin by saying 'excuse me' or 'hello'. At other times you will find that someone will ask you a question or make a comment. This usually means they want a conversation with you.

2 Smile. Use a pleasant voice.

3 Look at their face and turn your body towards them. Follow up on what they have said, or say something about what is happening around you.

4 Take turns to listen and to speak. A conversation is about sharing, and this means staying on the topic.

5 Conversations flow more easily when connectors and comments are used (hold up a set of CONVERSATION CARDS and mention each student will

receive their own set soon). Connectors such as, 'Why did you do that?' 'Where did you find it?' and 'What did you do next?' invite the other person to say more. Similarly, comments such as, 'I like that', 'I wish I could have been there' and 'I agree with you' help to follow up on what the other person has said.

6   Keep judging the other person's interest in the conversation. If they seem uninterested politely bring it to an end.

(Write these six steps on the whiteboard or butcher's paper)

Just as there is a recipe to make a conversation sparkle, there is also a recipe to wreck conversations. Do you know some of the ingredients?

Ingredients to wreck a conversation

- Constantly disagree.
- Say mean things about others.
- Go on and on about what you like.
- Don't talk and don't join in.
- Brag.
- Be grumpy.
- Interrupt.
- Jump to new topics all the time.
- Talk so much that others can't get a word in.
- Tune out and walk away – that's rude!

(Write 'How to wreck a conversation' on the whiteboard or butcher's paper)

2. Show me the Buzz

Show me the Buzz gives students the opportunity to practise and show they understand the new skill set. Hand out a set of 'conversation connectors' and 'conversation comments' to each student (located at the end of the chapter).

Break the group into pairs.

In this activity one student will start the conversation. The person starting the conversation has the choice of topic. Suggest that each pair sits on the floor facing one another with their 'conversation connectors' and 'conversation comments' in front of them. By doing this they can use them as a prompt to maintain a lively conversation. Remind the participants to show interest by using friendly faces and bodies.

Give pairs time to practise their conversational skills. Help out where you need to.

Next, encourage each pair to perform their sparkling conversation in front of the group. Use a stop watch to see if participants can keep a conversation flowing naturally for sixty seconds. Most revel in this, and the others in the group always enjoy watching and giving feedback!

If time permits repeat the activity with the other partner beginning the conversation.

3. Do you know the Buzz?

Do you know the Buzz? is a fast-moving question time. Its purpose is to consolidate the concepts gathered in the lesson. Encourage everyone to have a go. Here is the challenge.

Decide which statements are true, false or confusing. Put your thumbs up if you think the statement is true, thumbs down if you think the statement is false and put your thumbs to the side if you think the statement should be challenged.

Round 1

The best skills to make a conversation sparkle are to:

- laugh loudly all the time

- use a big voice so everyone knows you're the boss

- share talking time as evenly as you can

- give good eye contact

- put others down so you look good

- look sulky, grumpy and put out

- talk only about the things you are interested in

- use a few conversation connectors and conversation comments

- watch the other person so you can judge their interest in the conversation

- stand or sit at about an arm's length away from the person you're speaking to

- go on and on about how much you've got and where you've been

- show you are interested by leaning slightly forward, smiling, nodding and contributing

- get the timing right – always think, 'Is this a good time for this person to have a conversation?'

3. The Buzz

During *The Buzz* students play games that help them to practise their newly learned skills.

Talk, Listen, Cooperate and Create (passive for all ages)

This game asks the group to work together and arrange their bodies into a particular shape by lying on the floor. Stand on a chair or a desk to gain some height and added perspective. Remind the group that to solve each of the problems together effectively they will need to listen, talk with one another, share ideas and cooperate. There is no time limit. It is your decision as to whether the shape meets the standard or needs to be reworked.

The best way to start is to draw a picture of the shape required on the whiteboard. Ideal shapes to begin with are:

- a circle

- a triangle

- a square

- the letter A

- the letter B

- a heart

- a figure eight

- perpendicular lines

- parallel lines

- a wave

- a star

- a spiral.

Talking about Henny's Coloured Eggs (exciting for all ages)

One player is chosen to be the sneaky fox. One player is chosen to be Henny the Hen. The rest of the players are Henny's coloured chicks.

Put the fox on the far side of the room. Henny the Hen gives a colour to each chick by whispering it into their ears. The chicks line up behind Henny. Henny faces the fox in the middle of the room.

The fox creeps up to Henny and stands in front of her. It pretends to knock on the chicken pen door. Older students love to ham the conversation up!

Henny responds, 'Who is it?'

The fox replies, 'It's me, the fox.'

Henny says, 'What do you want?'

The fox says, 'Coloured chicks, yummy, yummy!'

Henny says, 'I haven't got any.'

At this moment all chicks giggle.

The fox says,'I hear them laughing.'

'Maybe I have got some,' says Henny, 'What colour do you want.'

The fox begins to guess colours. When it guesses a colour that has been given to a chick the little chick runs for its life to the far side of the room touching a wall.

If the fox catches the chick before it makes it safely to the wall a new game begins. If the fox doesn't catch the chick the same game is restarted, but this chick is now safe!

Stand in the Line (passive for all ages)

Players are required to form lines according to:

- height, shortest to tallest
- hair colour, lightest to darkest
- eye colour, lightest to darkest
- Christian names, alphabetically
- dates of birth, youngest to oldest
- size of feet, smallest to longest
- size of middle finger, smallest to longest
- widest smile, shortest to widest.

Encourage players to talk and look for consensus. There is no time limit. Once players are ready they simply hold up their hands!

5. *Goodbye Buzz*

Bid students a warm goodbye and remind them to take their folders, which contain:

- a copy of this lesson for parents

- a copy of *After the Buzz: social thinking ideas for parents*

- the 'conversational cards'.

As feedback for thoughtful behaviours each student may leave with a small gift.

After the Buzz: social thinking ideas for parents

Lesson 14: The Connecting Art of Conversation

In this lesson your child learned the vital skills about the art of conversation. As well, they had an opportunity to practise.

What is interesting is that when these skills are broken down into individual components we quickly realise that conversation relies heavily on a myriad of small, intricate skills such as:

- timing

- looking

- listening

- physical proximity

- reading the body language of another

- judging their interest

- appropriate topic selection

- conversation connecting abilities

- compromise

- patience

- assertiveness

- confidence.

With so many skills linked to good conversation, it is not surprising that for those already wrestling with one developmental issue or another, the art of conversation will take longer to master. Below is a selection of ideas for parents to develop their children's conversational skills.

- Be the best role model you can

- When your child converses with you try to display the simple things that you expect from them; stop what you are doing, give eye contact, listen carefully, respond to questions, connect ideas and exchange thoughts. As our children observe our well developed conversational skills in action we positively drip-feed their emerging skills.

- Make time for conversation

  After all, practice makes perfect. Many families earmark an evening meal each day for this purpose, others make use of car trips or the time it takes to walk home from school or go to the shops. Try to create opportunities to converse; make them part of the daily or weekly routine.

- The need to be deliberate

  Children who are the focus of *What's the Buzz?* are dependent on precise training that teaches them how to think socially and transfer that thinking into everyday practice. The deliberate guidance, coaching and development of foundation skills are crucial in order for some to achieve mastery. The action taken by James' parents in the case study below illustrates this very point.

  Case study, stretching James' conversational skills

  James was excitable and just wouldn't stop talking at the dinner table. Every evening he gave an exhaustive commentary on what had happened to him throughout the day. In the space of thirty minutes while his family sat eating, most of the talk time was commandeered by eleven-year-old James. But, a three-minute timer changed this forever! There were five people sitting at the table, and talk time needed to be evenly divided to allow conversation. It was decided that each person had to be guaranteed three minutes of uninterrupted talk time. When it was not their turn, they could ask questions of the person speaking, and when they had nothing to say they gave the remainder of their time to someone else. The new system helped James to regulate his talk time, gave him the opportunity to listen and ensured others had scope to participate. These days James is still long-winded, but when his parents say – 'summarise it James' – he understands.

- Four ideas to raise your child's conversational skills

  Idea 1

  Go shopping with your child and purchase an inexpensive wallet. Slip the 'conversation cards' from this lesson into it. Keep them in the two categories; 'conversation connectors' and 'conversation comments'.

  To play take all the cards out and place them on the floor so you can both see them. Choose a topic and start a conversation. Have fun choosing card after card to help the conversation progress. Physically point to cards you think will be useful in keeping the conversation flowing. Occasionally, deliberately choose a card that you know will not work and see if your child catches you out by offering better advice. This is fun and the practice will assist them to build conversational flexibility and confidence.

  Idea 2

  In this week's lesson your child learned the skills to make conversations sparkle. The positive steps on 'how to make a conversation sparkle' are in the lesson. Also in the lesson were a set of tips on 'Ingredients to wreck a conversation'.

Ingredients to wreck a conversation

- Constantly disagree.
- Say mean things about others.
- Go on and on about what you like.
- Don't talk and don't join in.
- Brag.
- Be grumpy.
- Interrupt.
- Jump to new topics all the time.
- Talk so much that others can't get a word in.
- Tune out and walking away – that's rude!

We offer these as a discussion and reference point.

Idea 3

Every so often brainstorm the set of skills needed to maintain a sparkling conversation:

- timing
- looking
- listening
- physical proximity
- reading the body language of another
- judging their interest
- appropriate topic selection
- conversation connecting abilities
- compromise
- assertiveness
- confidence, and many more.

Display this list on a large piece of poster paper and fasten pictures from magazines to show the required skills. Place the poster on show for everyone in the family to see!

Idea 4

Sensitively arrange opportunities for your child to practise their newly acquired conversational skills, especially when there isn't the pressure of making mistakes in front of peers. One idea may be to organise your child to catch up with a friend or relative who is sensitive to your child's needs. They might sit with your child and talk, knowing your child is in the process of strengthening their conversational skills.

Photocopiable resources now follow, and don't forget the online resources at www.whatsthebuzz.net.au!

What's the Buzz?

Conversation connectors

Conversation connectors invite the other person to say more. They make the conversation flow more easily.

What's the Buzz?

Conversation Connectors

Why?

Why did you do that?

Why did you go there?

Why did you want it?

What's the Buzz?

Conversation Connectors

What else?

What did that feel like?

What did you do?

What do you know about it?

What's the Buzz?

Conversation Connectors

Where?

Where did you find it?

Where did you get it?

Where did you go?

What's the Buzz?

Conversation Connectors

How?

How did you get there?

How did you end up doing that?

How did that happen?

What's the Buzz?

Conversation Connectors

What?

What did you do there?

What did she say next?

What did you do next?

What's the Buzz?

Conversation Connectors

When?

When did you go there?

When did you see it?

When did you see him/her?

What's the Buzz?

Conversation comments

Conversation comments highlight something another person has said.

What's the Buzz?

Conversation Comments

I also . . .

I also like that

I also want that

I also saw that

What's the Buzz?

Conversation Comments

I agree . . .

I agree with what you are saying

I agree with what you did

I agree with you

What's the Buzz?

Conversation Comments

I wish . . .

I wish I could do that

I wish I could have been there

I wish I could have seen it

What's the Buzz?

Conversation Comments

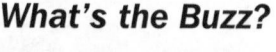

I like . . .

I like that

I like those

I like going there too

What's the Buzz?

Conversation Comments

I have . . .

I have one of those

I have something like that

I have felt like that before

Learning to 'Fit in'

Explanation

As *What's the Buzz?* draws to a close it is opportune to remind practitioners and parents about the motivations behind this social development programme. It is inspired by the deep admiration we have for so many of the participants we work alongside. Can you imagine having to interact in a socially and emotionally rich world, yet struggle to be socially flexible; to interpret one's own feelings, to process them smoothly and efficiently, to understand the feelings of others and react aptly? This is what confronts so many of the children and adolescents we work with as they do their best to belong and find friendship.

Typically, many struggle with a fundamental skill: *social referencing*. That is, the ability to watch and gauge what others are doing, and then use the information as a practical reference to pitch their own behaviour. Social referencing refers to a set of skills required to *fit in* and usually begins to strengthen quite early in the lives of most children. It is driven by the need to be accepted and experience satisfying social connections. Those who are unable to socially reference often face an assortment of complex difficulties:

• Poor impulse control

'Busy. Too active and too reactive to tune into what is happening. They must tell all and get on to the next thing!'

• Anxiety

'Nervous. Too worried about surviving the moment to notice what is really happening around them.'

• Low confidence

'Feel as though their efforts will not be good enough. Worry about disapproval or rejection and how to handle it.'

• An inflated view of their own importance

'An exaggerated view that the world works around them and should fit in with them.'

- Socially immature

    'Wants to fit in and shows intermittent signs of this. However, is easily socially overloaded resulting in silly or defensive behaviours.'

- Global developmental delay

    'Does not know how to socially reference and has not yet perceived the need or value.'

The aim of this lesson is to teach students how to use other people's actions and energy as a compass to monitor their own behaviour. It is to coach participants that others supply each of us with important information about the behaviours that are acceptable and expected at particular times. Once we begin to observe and pick up on these cues we provide ourselves with the best chance to regulate our behaviour and make it socially appropriate.

The lesson also begins to explore the concept of self-awareness. As students start to appreciate their natural style, and the inherent challenges, they place themselves in a position ready to make changes and do things differently.

Materials required for Lesson 15

- Whiteboard/butcher's paper and a marker

- Post *What's the Buzz?* group rules (located on p. 20; alternatively, they can be downloaded from www.whatsthebuzz.net.au)

- Place an outline of the lesson on the whiteboard/butcher's paper

- Photocopy four copies of The skit (contained within the lesson)

- Two copies of each 'Self-awareness questionnaire': 'School challenges' and 'Family challenges' for each student (located in the photocopiable resources at the end of this lesson; alternatively, they can be downloaded from www.whatsthebuzz.net.au)

- One stapler

- Print one 'POST-GROUP social functioning survey' for parents, one for teachers and one for students to complete (located in the photocopiable resources at the end of this lesson; alternatively, they can be downloaded from www.whatsthebuzz.net.au)

- A reminder note to parents; as the next lesson is our last, a plate of food to share would be appreciated

- One marker and several A3 sheets of paper for the game 'Dare to dream?'

- Photocopy the set of 'Red letter alphabet cards' (located in the photocopiable resources at the end of this lesson; alternatively, they can be downloaded from www.whatsthebuzz.net.au)

- Organise the gold nuggets, cubes to build a friendship wall, group rule and reminder cards or a similar feedback device (see the chapter, Practical Considerations)

- A small gift for each child

- Prepare handouts for parent(s):

  - One copy of this lesson for each parent to read
  - One copy of *After the Buzz: social thinking ideas for parents* for each parent to read (section follows this lesson).

Lesson 15

Arrange participants into a social circle. Welcome them.

Draw everyone's attention to the group rules. Display the feedback device to encourage positive social behaviours (see section on feedback ideas in the chapter, Practical Considerations). Explain that if successful each student may leave with a small gift.

1. What's the Buzz?

What's the Buzz? introduces students to this lesson's topic and the new set of skills to be learned.

Explain that this lesson is about 'social referencing'. It is the skill of learning how to 'fit in', socially. Without it, it is hard to find friends and be accepted. To do this each of us must learn to stop, watch what is happening, work out what others are doing and match our behaviour with theirs. To work successfully with others we have to gather every bit of information. It is the same as getting dressed in the morning. We know how we should dress when we are having a run of hot days. We would feel uncomfortable, and probably look strange, if we arrived at school wearing a jumper, a thick coat, a scarf, gloves, woolly socks and boots!

The skit

Arrange participants to watch the following. Ask them to think about the actions of Caitlin. How would they rate her social referencing skills?

Allow the actors to introduce themselves and the characters they are playing.

Caitlin:	'Let's play chess! Come on!' (bursts into the room grabbing Matisse who is quietly reading. Pulls Matisse roughly by the arm on to the floor and hastily unpacks a chess set ready to play)
Matisse:	(closing her book) 'Well, okay. I'm not that good, but I can play.'
Caitlin:	'I want to play and I'm good!' (rubbing her hands together)
Matisse:	(worried look on face) 'Okay. Let's play, but just for fun'
Caitlin:	'I'm a total legend at this' (then spells out L-E-G-E-N-D loudly and excitedly)
Matisse:	(starts to look annoyed) 'Yeah, yeah, yeah. Let's play.'
Caitlin:	'Get ready to be wiped out! This is my kind of game!' (continuing to be loud and excited)
Matisse:	(moves back from the board) 'You know, I don't feel like playing anymore.'

Caitlin: 'That's pathetic! You don't want to play because you know you'll lose.'

Matisse: (speaking confidently) 'Actually I don't want to play because I'm tired of you going on and on and bragging' (gets up and walks away with her book).

Applause

Following the applause turn to the group and ask:

- Did Caitlin match her behaviour with the behaviour of Matisse?

- What did Caitlin forget to do?

- When we forget to 'tune in' and work out what is happening around us, what is likely to happen?

- Let's replay this. Who would like to take the role of Caitlin and show us how to make this work successfully? Let's see if we can find two or three successful ways to do this?

2. Show me the Buzz

Show me the Buzz gives students the opportunity to practise and show they understand the new skill set. Arrange the group into a social circle. Pose this question: 'Who understands the challenges they face at home and school?'

Let's do a quick survey.

Put your hand up if you know you are challenged by:

- being poorly organised?

- not getting work finished at school?

- being too shy with others?

- getting angry too fast?

- having to be the boss?

- accepting 'no' from parents?

- accepting 'no' from teachers?

- wanting to have your own way too often?

- poor concentration?

- getting grumpy over homework most nights?

- being too fidgety or restless?

- losing games?

- being too loud?

- being too shy?

- worrying too much?

As we start to understand our challenges we are more likely to try new ways to do things.

The best idea is to experiment with small changes that take you in a better direction.

Self-awareness questionnaires

This activity requires everyone to complete two Self-awareness questionnaires: 'School challenges' and 'Family challenges'.

Each questionnaire highlights the things many students have trouble with. They are quick to fill in and students usually enjoy discussing their choices. As participants finish up congratulate them on appreciating more about their natural style and taking a step to become more self-aware.

Finally, hand each student two blank questionnaires, 'School challenges' and 'Family challenges', and staple each to the sheets they have just filled out. Suggest they ask their class teacher (optional) and parents to fill out the blank ones. This will provide them with a chance to compare their ratings with the ratings of significant others in their life.

Impress on everyone that they are not to see Mum's, Dad's or their teacher's feedback as wrong or right if it is different to theirs. Instead, try to see any differences as a precious opportunity to learn more about their 'social referencing'; how others see them fitting in. Assist participants to place the completed and blank questionnaires into their folder.

3. Do you know the Buzz?

Do you know the Buzz? is a fast-moving question time. Its purpose is to consolidate the essence of the lesson.

Arrange the group into a social circle. Ask participants to listen carefully as they hear a series of rapid-fire statements. Their challenge is to decide whether the statement is true or false. If they believe it is true they are to put their thumbs up. If they think it is false they are to put their thumbs down and if they think a statement should be challenged they need to place their thumbs to the side. Good luck. Here we go!

Round 1

To give yourself the best chance to 'fit in':

- always check what other people are doing before you do anything

- switch your voice and noise level to match what is happening around you

- switch your behaviour to match what most others are doing around you

- be funny so people will like you

- do whatever you feel like doing whenever you feel like doing it

- put on your best sulky face to get what you want

- bully others to get your way

- work out what the group is doing and try and do things in the same way

- work out what the group is doing and do the opposite

- push your way in – be bossy

- wait, look, listen and tune in – then you'll know what's happening

- copy the behaviours of the kids who are liked and respected.

4. The Buzz

During *The Buzz* students play games that help strengthen the skills central to the lesson. The more group members are encouraged to play these, and similar games, the more opportunity they have to generalise their social thinking and social skills into their day-to-day interactions.

Red Letter (exciting for all ages)

Use the set of 'Red letter alphabet cards' located at the end of this lesson. Ideally, a large grassed area, a basketball court or a large room is best to play this game.

Line players across a start line and explain that you will randomly draw one 'Red letter alphabet card' at a time. As each letter is drawn and called out players may take one giant step forward if that letter is in their Christian name. The first person to the finish line wins. The game continues until everyone has crossed the finish line.

There are some amusing variations to the game. Instead of asking players to take one giant step forward each time a letter is called, ask them to:

- hop

- kangaroo jump

- jump and spin, or

- get them to lie on the ground and roll over just once.

As students participate remind them to observe how others are playing the game. Is everyone doing what is expected? Are they following the instructions? This game, like most, concerns 'social referencing' and for the game to work each person needs to watch what is happening, work out how the others are playing and match their behaviour to the group.

Guess What I'm Drawing? (passive for all ages)

Give each player a turn to be an artist and draw a picture on the whiteboard or butcher's paper. Ask them to decide on a simple image to draw before they volunteer. Basic drawings such as fruit and vegetables are fine! It is a good idea to get the player to whisper in your ear what they intend to draw.

As their drawing develops, others in the group will raise their hands when they think they know what it is. The artist stops drawing to choose someone. However, they can only respond by saying 'yes' or 'no'. The artist may need to continue to draw to give more clues. The person who guesses is offered the next turn.

Dare to Dream? (passive for older students)

Ask if someone is prepared to share an ambition or dream they hope to achieve one day. Write their ambition on to butcher's paper or an A3 size sheet of paper and add their name to it.

Clarify there are two things to keep in mind as they chase their ambition. Draw a horizontal line under their name and ambition, and connect a vertical line to it so the page is divided into halves. At the top of one column write the heading, ACCELERATORS (*positive things* that boost opportunities for success – helpful attitudes, supportive friends, a realistic vision, being organised, accepting responsibility, having a homework routine, good relationship with Mum and Dad, aware of personal strengths, etc.). At the top of the other column write OBSTACLES (*negative things* that will spoil opportunities for success – negative feelings, poor friendship choices, dislike of school, inability to compromise, poorly organised, fighting with parents etc.). Explain to students what these terms mean and the importance of understanding them.

Next ask students to brainstorm ideas under both headings. You will be amazed at how they are able to identify ACCELERATORS and OBSTACLES so clearly for others. Aim at about half a dozen ideas for each column. Once finished, give the sheet of paper to the volunteer to take home. If time permits do another! However, be prepared for each student to have one of these blueprints for the future completed for them.

5. Goodbye Buzz

Bid students a warm goodbye and remind them to take their folders, which contain:

- a copy of this lesson for parents

- a copy of *After the Buzz: social thinking ideas for parents*

- a completed 'Self-awareness questionnaire: School challenges' and a blank one for teacher to fill in (optional)

- a completed 'Self-awareness questionnaire: Family challenges' and a blank one for parents to fill in

- a 'TEACHER FORM: post-group social functioning survey', a 'PARENT FORM: post-group social functioning survey' and a 'STUDENT FORM: post-group social functioning survey'

- a reminder note to parents about a plate of food to share.

As feedback for thoughtful behaviours each student may leave with a small gift.

After the Buzz: social thinking ideas for parents

Lesson 15: Learning to 'Fit in'

The focus of this lesson was to teach participants the skills required to 'fit in' with others more successfully. This hinges heavily on one's ability to watch, gauge what others are doing and use the information as a guide to pitch their own behaviour. As we explicitly teach children how to 'socially reference' or 'fit in' we also offer them a design to stretch their self-awareness and improve relationships with family and community. Here are a few carefully selected ideas parents may wish to follow up on at home to strengthen their children's ability to social reference.

- Expectations, structures and routines

  Children who struggle to 'fit in' are advantaged by parents able to set up steady routines and sensible expectations. They depend on parents who give clear direction and provide ongoing feedback by catching the positive behaviours they value. This parenting style actively helps young people to tune in: to look, to listen, to remember, to follow instructions and actually get along with others. By maintaining consistency you offer your child a much greater chance to 'fit in'. Here is a sample of the challenges that regularly crop up for young people who struggle with social referencing:

  – 'Mum, can I bring this drink and bag of crisps to the social skills group?'

  – 'Can I take my big teddy bear to school each day?'

  – 'Why can't I use my mobile phone at the dinner table?'

  – 'Why do I have to help with the dishes?'

  – 'Why can't I have a television in my bedroom?'

  – 'Why do I have to watch what everyone else wants?'

  – 'Why won't my teacher let me read my novel in class when I want to?'

  – 'Why do I have to do homework?'

  – 'Dad, why can't I take my pocket knife to school?'

  – 'What's wrong with playing my computer games when I want to?'

- Family meetings

  Ever thought of running a family meeting each fortnight? It does not have to be a formal arrangement, but simply a forum to provide praise and develop new expectations. The essence of a family meeting is to review what is happening in the family, what is working and what is not. This forum provides everyone with a voice to discuss, review and make changes. Family meetings are an excellent vehicle to build relationships, model respect and demonstrate compromise. So often it's not making the rule that provides an advantage, but more the act of asking and participating together. Simple ideas that are workable and generally acceptable can make a world of difference.

- Be direct and help your child gather data

Deliberately pointing out what is happening and what is expected in particular situations is always helpful. For example, if your child has trouble being quiet in the library, then as you enter whisper, 'Look, everyone is working quietly. Reading and researching is quiet work' or, 'Libraries are quiet places. It makes it easier to concentrate.' If, on the other hand, there is a child in the library running about and making a lot of noise, whisper to your child how that behaviour does not match what everyone else is doing. Such comments help your child gather useful data that they may not easily reference independently.

- Always have a 'marker'

Tune your child into observing the appropriate behaviours of others so they can 'fit in' in and give themselves the best chance to find social success. Do what you can to connect them to the 'good guys'.

Example

Ten-year-old Sean had a reputation for losing things, forgetting and being dreadfully disorganised, but he stumbled across a simple solution worth sharing! Sean's solution was to start copying what one of his closest friends did. He began to stack his locker the same way as Claire stacked hers. He placed the same books on his desk as Claire each morning. He mimicked what Claire did in the classroom; from note-taking and organising his folder, to filling out his diary at the end of the day and making sure he bagged the same homework books. It wasn't a cure-all, but helped Sean to work at a functional level, and it felt so good! Engaging children to watch others with a view to imitating their strengths can be useful, even inspirational.

- Observe the behaviours of others

Observation is a powerful learning tool. One idea to tune children into noticing whether their actions and behaviours are similar to others is by list making. It is quick and this lighthearted approach is useful every so often. On a sheet of paper draw four columns. At the top of each column write headings as:

- 'the friendliest kids in class'
- 'the kids who just get on with their work'
- 'the kids the teacher likes the most'
- 'the helpful kids.'

Then ask your child to rank the children in class with the first named being the best in the category, and continue until their name is inserted on to the list. Ask, 'Is that where you want to be?' 'What can you do to change this?' Every so often review and update the lists. This approach offers insights into fitting in, stretches self-awareness, allows for new goals to be set and connects them to the behaviours of the children who do it well.

• Watch movies and sitcoms

As mentioned earlier, film is a perfect means to coach children how to 'fit in' and get along with others. By observing what works and doesn't work for others children receive a rich stream of information they can progressively apply to their own lives. Try discussing some of these ideas with your child to help them identify 'fitting-in' type behaviours:

– why were certain characters funny, loved, odd, disliked, or unhappy?
– what did they do that helped them fit in to the group?
– what did they do that annoyed others in the group?
– who was their favourite character and why?
– who was their least favourite character and why?
– what helped them to make this judgement?

Observing the behaviour of others in this way offers children the opportunity to see how social referencing works. It is also a safe teaching vehicle as the spotlight is not directly on them.

• The questionnaires: 'school challenges' and 'family challenges'

These should be in your child's folder. The blank questionnaire, 'School challenges' can be completed by your son or daughter's teacher (this is optional based on how they feel about their teacher's input) and the other, 'Family challenges', can be completed by you. The idea is for students to compare their questionnaire responses with the responses of trusted others. There is no wrong or right here; this is a valuable opportunity for children to learn more about themselves through understanding how others see them. Use the differences as a basis for a constructive discussion. Perhaps there is something that can be targeted as a new goal to pursue at home or school.

Photocopiable resources now follow, and don't forget the online resources at www.whatsthebuzz.net.au!

After the Buzz . . . Lesson 15

What's the Buzz?

Teacher form

POST-GROUP social functioning survey

Child's name _____ Date _____

Teacher's name _____ Phone _____

School _____ Age/year level _____

Circle the number displayed with each question or statement that 'feels about right' based on your observations.
Also, please circle any key words in the questions and statements that highlight a particular concern.

1 = no/never   2 = hardly ever/a bit   3 = mostly/a lot   4 = certainly/yes

1. Is the student accepted by peers?
   1   2   3   4
2. Do you think this student has the desire to make friends?
   1   2   3   4
3. Does the student notice the behaviours of others and try to 'fit in' with them?
   1   2   3   4
4. The student looks for relationships, but is unsuccessful
   1   2   3   4
5. Do you think this student is happy enough, socially?
   1   2   3   4
6. This student understands how to 'read' and respond to the emotions of others
   1   2   3   4
7. Does the student deal with conflict and disagreements between peers appropriately?
   1   2   3   4
8. The student follows instructions and completes tasks appropriately
   1   2   3   4
9. Does the student have learning difficulties/a short attention span or is distractible?
   1   2   3   4
10. This student displays (circle appropriate words) anger, crying, sulking, shyness, hitting, running away, biting, withdrawing, verbal abuse when things go wrong?
    1   2   3   4
11. I have seen benefits arising from this student's participation in the programme
    1   2   3   4

Please mention benefits here _____

_____

The information you have shared may be viewed by the student's parents.
Please return as soon as possible. **Thank you!**

What's the Buzz?

Parent form

POST-GROUP social functioning survey

Child's name _____   Date _____

Parent's name _____   Phone _____

School _____   Age/year level _____

Circle the number displayed with each question or statement that 'feels about right' based on your observations.

Also, please circle any key words in the questions and statements that highlight a particular concern.

1 = no/never   **2 = hardly ever/a bit**   **3 = mostly/a lot**   **4 = certainly/yes**

1. Does your child have friends at school?
         1   2   3   4

2. Do you think they have the ability/ desire to make friends and be a friend?
         1   2   3   4

3. My child is able to establish relationships, maintain them and enjoy them
         1   2   3   4

4. My child is able to 'fit in' with others and 'go with the flow'
         1   2   3   4

5. My child is happy with their own company. They do not seek relationships with others
         1   2   3   4

6. My child reads the emotions and feelings of others suitably
         1   2   3   4

7. My child handles disagreements and conflicts constructively
         1   2   3   4

8. My child has a short attention span, is often distracted and is very active
         1   2   3   4

9. My child has enjoyed *What's the Buzz?*
         1   2   3   4

10. My child is prone to (circle appropriate words) anger, crying, sulking, shyness, hitting, running away, biting, withdrawing, verbal abuse when things go wrong?
         1   2   3   4

11. I have seen benefits arising from my child's participation in the programme?
         1   2   3   4

Please mention benefits here _____

_____

The information you have shared may be viewed by your child's teacher.
Please return as soon as possible. **Thank you!**

What's the Buzz?

Student form

POST-GROUP social functioning survey

Your name _____ Age/year level _____

Teacher's name/class _____ School _____

Circle the number below each question that 'feels right' to you

Remember, there are no right or wrong answers. We want to find out if anything has changed since starting What's the Buzz?

1 = no/never   2 = hardly ever/a bit   3 = mostly/a lot   4 = certainly/yes

1. Do you have friends to play with at school?
   1   2   3   4
2. Are you liked by children?
   1   2   3   4
3. Once you make a friend, do you happily keep the friendship?
   1   2   3   4
4. Do you get too excited, too silly or too bossy around other children?
   1   2   3   4
5. Do you feel too shy or worried to make friends?
   1   2   3   4
6. Do you get confused trying to work out the feelings of other kids?
   1   2   3   4
7. Do you get so annoyed when someone is mean to you that you handle it badly?
   1   2   3   4
8. Is it easy to talk to children your own age and get along with them?
   1   2   3   4
9. Is it hard to concentrate and get your work done at school?
   1   2   3   4
10. When things go wrong do you get very upset? Do you cry, sulk, get angry or hurt others?
    1   2   3   4
11. I think *What's the Buzz?* has been helpful   yes / no
    I have enjoyed *What's the Buzz?*   yes / no

What's the Buzz? has helped me to _____

_____

_____

If you want help to do this survey ask Mum, Dad, your teacher or your What's the Buzz? facilitator. This information may be seen by your parents or teacher.

Please return as soon as you can. Thank you!

What's the Buzz?

Red letter alphabet cards

What's the Buzz? **A** Red letter alphabet	*What's the Buzz?* **B** Red letter alphabet	*What's the Buzz?* **C** Red letter alphabet	*What's the Buzz?* **D** Red letter alphabet
What's the Buzz? **E** Red letter alphabet	*What's the Buzz?* **F** Red letter alphabet	*What's the Buzz?* **G** Red letter alphabet	*What's the Buzz?* **H** Red letter alphabet
What's the Buzz? **I** Red letter alphabet	*What's the Buzz?* **J** Red letter alphabet	*What's the Buzz?* **K** Red letter alphabet	*What's the Buzz?* **L** Red letter alphabet
What's the Buzz? **M** Red letter alphabet	*What's the Buzz?* **N** Red letter alphabet	*What's the Buzz?* **O** Red letter alphabet	*What's the Buzz?* **P** Red letter alphabet
What's the Buzz? **Q** Red letter alphabet	*What's the Buzz?* **R** Red letter alphabet	*What's the Buzz?* **S** Red letter alphabet	*What's the Buzz?* **T** Red letter alphabet
What's the Buzz? **U** Red letter alphabet	*What's the Buzz?* **V** Red letter alphabet	*What's the Buzz?* **W** Red letter alphabet	*What's the Buzz?* **X** Red letter alphabet
What's the Buzz? **Y** Red letter alphabet	*What's the Buzz?* **Z** Red letter alphabet		

What's the Buzz?

Self-awareness questionnaire: school challenges

Lots of students have trouble with these things at school. Do you? Rate these according to the trouble they cause you.

Name: _____

1. Talking in class

That's trouble	Mostly	Sometimes	No trouble

2. Sitting still and concentrating in class

That's trouble	Mostly	Sometimes	No trouble

3. Distracting others in class

I always do that	Mostly	Sometimes	I never do that

4. Finishing work in lesson

I never finish	Sometimes	Mostly	I always finish

5. Doing what the teacher asks me to do

That's trouble	Mostly	Sometimes	No trouble

6. My learning

That's always hard	Mostly	Sometimes	Never hard

7. Getting along with other kids

That's trouble	Mostly	Sometimes	No trouble

8. Finishing off work set over a long period

That's trouble	Mostly	Sometimes	No trouble

What's the Buzz?

Self-awareness questionnaire: family challenges

Lots of kids have trouble with these things at home. Do you? Rate these according to the trouble they cause you

Name: _____

1. Getting out of bed in the morning without reminding

That's trouble	Mostly	Sometimes	No trouble

2. Getting ready for school by myself and on time

That's trouble	Mostly	Sometimes	No trouble

3. Getting my homework done by myself

That's trouble	Mostly	Sometimes	No trouble

4. Keeping my bedroom tidy

That's trouble	Mostly	Sometimes	No trouble

5. Remembering chores and jobs

That's trouble	Mostly	Sometimes	No trouble

6. Going to bed on time and staying in bed

That's trouble	Mostly	Sometimes	No trouble

7. Remembering to help Mum or Dad with those little jobs

Always forget	Mostly forget	Sometimes forget	Never forget

8. Watching too much television or playing computer games for too long

That's trouble	Mostly	Sometimes	Never

Giving and Receiving Compliments

Explanation

Welcome to the last lesson of *What's the Buzz?*

Is giving a compliment important? Absolutely! Sadly, most of us give and receive too few, but the delightful response a compliment brings reminds us just how valuable they really are.

When we give compliments we let others see we appreciate them for who they are or for what they have done. The truth is people generally look for and like reassuring and positive feedback. Indeed, the behavioural experts have long told us that optimistic feedback, such as giving a compliment, positively influences the attitudes and behaviours of others towards us.

This lesson examines what a compliment is, why it is a good idea to compliment others, how to deliver compliments and how to receive them.

It looks at their versatile role in day-to-day interaction because they can be used to cheer someone up, to start a conversation, but also have the scope to build warmth and loyalty in an established friendship. Teaching children how to pay a compliment and how to respond to a compliment adds a valuable layer of social thinking to the skills they have learned throughout the programme.

Materials required for Lesson 16

- Whiteboard/butcher's paper and a marker

- Post *What's the Buzz?* group rules (located on p. 20; alternatively, they can be downloaded from www.whatsthebuzz.net.au)

- Place an outline of the lesson on the whiteboard/butcher's paper

- Purchase or make one greeting card for each participant. It is best to purchase the same card for each student and make sure the centre is blank so students have plenty of room to write

- One rug and two medium-sized skipping ropes for the game 'All In'

- In this lesson children have been asked to bring a plate of food for each to share. You may wish to supply drinks

- Prepare a Certificate of Graduation for each student (located in the photocopiable resources at the end of this lesson; alternatively, they can be downloaded from www.whatsthebuzz.net.au)

- Organise the gold nuggets, cubes to build a friendship wall, group rule and reminder cards or a similar feedback device (see the chapter, Practical Considerations)

- Organise a small gift or a reward token for each child

- Prepare handouts for parent(s):

  - One copy of this lesson for each parent to read
  - One copy of *After the Buzz: social thinking ideas for parents* for each parent to read (section follows this lesson).

Lesson 16

Arrange participants into a social circle and welcome them to the last lesson. Announce that each participant will receive a *'What's the Buzz?* Certificate of Graduation to mark the end of the programme. These will be handed out later in the lesson. Draw everyone's attention to the group rules. Display the feedback device to encourage positive social behaviours (see section on feedback ideas in the chapter, Practical Considerations). Explain that if successful each student will leave with a small gift.

Collect 'TEACHER FORM: post-group social functioning survey' and 'PARENT FORM: post-group social functioning survey'.

1. What's the Buzz?

What's the Buzz? introduces students to this lesson's topic and the new set of skills to be learned.

Start by engaging eye contact with a participant and delivering a warm compliment to them. Wait for a moment to see how they respond to the compliment, and then move on.

Once each participant has received a compliment from you ask, 'What is it I have just done?' Next, reveal the definition of a compliment (write it on the whiteboard or butcher's paper).

> *A compliment is a kind word said about another person to show you have recognised a good quality in them.*
> (Oxford on-line Dictionary, retrieved February, 2010)

Ask:

- 'Why is it a good idea to compliment others?'

- 'Why is it a good idea to learn how to receive a compliment?'

Give students time to discuss these questions.

To conclude, use their ideas to complete the following and record them on the whiteboard or butcher's paper.

- It is a good idea to compliment others because . . .

- It is a good idea to receive a compliment kindly because . . .

Giving a compliment: *what to do*

- Be caring and truthful. Make it simple.

- Look at the person, smile and use a friendly voice.

- Keep the compliment to what has happened or something about that person.

- When you agree with someone else's positive opinion that is also a way to compliment.

- You can give a compliment in front of others or privately.

(Write 'Giving a compliment: *what to do'* on to the whiteboard or butcher's paper)

Receiving a compliment: *what to do*

- Smile, look at the person and always say 'thank you' because a compliment is a gift.

- Use a friendly voice.

- You can make your response longer:

  - 'Thank you for saying that, it means a lot'.

  - 'Thank you. That's a nice thing to say.'

  - 'I appreciate you telling me that. Thanks.'

- If you can, give a compliment back to them.

- Use the compliment as a way to start a conversation.

(Write 'Receiving a compliment: *what to do'* on to the whiteboard or butcher's paper)

2. Show me the Buzz

Show me the Buzz gives students the opportunity to practise and show they understand the new skill set. Arrange the group into a social circle.

Compliment cards

Hand each person a greeting card. When they open it they will find a compliment specifically written to each of them by you. For example, 'Dear Estelle, thanks for coming along to *What's the Buzz?* I like the way you have listened and have been such fun to be with.'

Next, ask each participant to pass their card to the person on their left. The task is for each student to write a compliment on each card. Continue to pass the cards around the circle until everyone has written a compliment on each person's card. Remind participants to put their name next to the compliment they write. Some students will find it difficult to think of a compliment because it is not something they are accustomed to giving. To help, provide the following list of compliments on the whiteboard or butcher's paper.

- You are always friendly.

- You often have clever ideas.

- You make people smile.

- I like how trustworthy you are.

- I like how you say what you think.

- You are great to be around.

- You've always been friendly to me.

- You say really clever things.

- I like how you think.

- I liked it when you . . .

- You are an honest person.

- You're a great listener.

- You're a good thinker.

- You are really funny.

- You are always fun to be with.

Watch out for students who struggle with writing and spelling; they may need your support.

Once students receive their card back give them time to read and enjoy the compliments written by the others. Invite participants to read them out. Usually, there's a degree of embarrassment over this, but once started it's delightful to watch the joyful expressions on each child's face as they read and absorb the compliments written for them.

Next, ask if anyone would like to respond to any of the compliments they have received. They can respond to an individual or to the group. Ask if anyone would like to explain why they wrote a particular comment to someone.

Have students place their 'compliment card' safely into their folder. The 'compliment card' is a precious reminder of the qualities group members have discovered about them. What a wonderful thing to look at the next time they need their spirits lifted!

3. Do you know the Buzz?

Do you know the Buzz? is a fast-moving question time. Its purpose is to consolidate the major concepts. Arrange the group so they are standing in a large social circle. Stand in the middle and invite them to watch carefully because their challenge is to decide whether the compliments you are about to give are sincere and caring or not. If they believe the compliment is genuine and well delivered they are to put their thumbs up. If they think the compliment is poorly delivered or is not a compliment they are to put their thumbs down. If they are not sure and want to challenge the idea they are to place their thumbs to the side. Let's go!

Round 1

Compliments: sincere and caring, or otherwise

- 'It's great to see you.' (genuine)

- 'It's great to see you.' (sarcastic, rolling eyes)

- 'You're really good at this.' (genuine)

- 'I love your haircut.' (genuine)

- 'You are such a good runner.' (mimicking a pigeon-toed runner)

- 'You make me laugh.' (genuine)

- 'You make me laugh. You're so funny. Everyone loves your jokes. You're fabulous!' (gushy and over the top)

- 'I really like your new car.' (genuine)

- 'I love your haircut.' (pulling a face, insincere and mocking)

- 'You're so funny.' (flat and fake)

- 'You played well in soccer today.' (turning away, shaking head and making a loser's sign on forehead)

- 'You are a brilliant artist.' (genuine)

- 'I like hanging out with you.' (genuine)

- 'You're such a great person to be around.' (genuine)

4. The Buzz

During *The Buzz* students play games that help them to practise their newly learned skills.

Ooh-Ahh (exciting for all ages)

Start with everyone sitting in a social circle holding hands. Nominate a player to give a 'quick squeeze' to the hand of the person on their left. This 'quick squeeze' is passed along to the next person and continues moving around the circle. Once the squeeze is being passed quickly and smoothly, speed it up and add sound. Each player must say 'Ooh' as they receive and pass on the 'quick squeeze'.

The game can be taken to a more complex level for older groups! Stop the squeeze running in the clockwise direction and start a new one that runs anticlockwise around the circle. Once the squeeze is being passed quickly and smoothly, speed it up and add a new sound. Each player must say 'Ahh' as they receive and pass on the 'quick squeeze'.

Next, try to run both squeezes together. To do this, start the 'Ooh's' on one side of the circle (running clockwise) and the 'Ahh's' on the other side (running anticlockwise). This is challenging, but great fun.

What I Like About You (passive for all ages)

Arrange the group to sit in a social circle. One person is chosen to be 'it' and they start by standing in the middle of the circle. 'It' approaches any player and says, 'What I really like about you is . . .'

Take a moment to revisit how a compliment is expected to be received. Ask one or two participants to give examples.

However, in this game there's a fun twist! The person receiving the compliment must NOT smile or giggle, but simply say, 'thank you' keeping a very straight face.

If they smile or giggle while responding they become 'it'. On the other hand, if they are able to keep a straight face, 'it' must approach a new person and try to make them smile. 'It' is not allowed to touch any of the players, but anything else is fair play.

All In (exciting)

This game asks students to communicate, cooperate, problem solve and show patience. It is great fun! Be warned: the game requires students to get physically close to one another. Mention this at the outset, and if a student wishes to sit out or observe, make it easy for them to do so.

To begin, lay a medium sized rug or blanket on the floor and ask the group to gather together and stand on it. No part of their bodies may touch the floor. Count out an official ten second count. Once the group has succeeded it's time to decrease the area, and increase the challenge! Ask them to step off the blanket for a moment and fold it in half. Restart the game. As the challenge becomes more difficult remind students to talk to one another, be helpful, move slowly and take their time. There is no time limit and they can restart over and over.

Next, fold the blanket in half again and see how the group works together to find a way to fit on and stay on for the ten second count. To increase the challenge make a circle by laying a small rope on the floor about half a metre away from the blanket the group is standing on. Ask them to gently move across and stand inside the circle without anyone touching the floor in the process (begin the ten second count as soon as they are all in the circle).

Want to test just how far your group can go? This time, place another rope circle (even smaller) next to the current rope circle and ask them to step across without anyone touching the floor. Wish them luck!

5. Goodbye Buzz

It's time to party together! Give students ten to fifteen minutes to share food, drink and say their goodbyes. If appropriate, encourage them to swap phone numbers, email or Facebook addresses so they can stay in touch with one another. Present *What's the Buzz?* Certificates of Graduation to each student and be sure to tell them something special you have noticed about their learning and progress.

Bid students a warm goodbye and remind them to take their folders, which contain:

- a copy of this lesson for parents

- a copy of *After the Buzz: social thinking ideas for parents*

- *What's the Buzz?* Certificates of Graduation

- their compliment cards.

As feedback for thoughtful behaviours each student may leave with a small gift.

After the Buzz: social thinking ideas for parents

Lesson 16: Giving and Receiving Compliments

As we reach the close of the programme let's take a moment to reflect on what is happening at home.

• Our influence

All children are reliant on the ideal role modelling of parents. However, children participating in *What's the Buzz?* are heavily reliant on the wisdom and patience of their parents. Parents who want to engage, who can create an emotionally supportive home life, and show their children how to make sense of the social and emotional world make such a difference. Rest assured, your care and persistence are the most potent forces in your child's life!

• Show how it's done

Be sure to compliment others when your children are about. Consistently set an appropriate standard for them to model their behaviours on. One idea is to help your children brainstorm a variety of compliments they could give to family members, friends and teachers. This increases the choices at their disposal. Here are a few ideas to begin with:

– 'You look nice today Mum.' (with or without a kiss)

– 'I'm glad you're home Dad.' (with or without a hug)

– 'Thanks for cooking dinner Mum/Dad.'

– 'Thanks for working so hard to earn money so we can have all the things we need.'

– 'Thanks for helping me with my homework.' (with a smile)

– 'It's great to see you.'

– 'I like being in your class.'

– 'That was great fun. Thanks!'

– 'You are a great Mum/Dad.'

– 'I'm glad you're my sister/brother.'

– 'I love you. You're the best.'

– 'I like the way you do that Mum/Dad.'

- Keep on complimenting your children

  Curiously, when our children are much younger and the milestones seem so many we develop the habit of giving regular positive feedback: learning to crawl, to use a spoon, walk, talk, run, hop, sing, read and write a word or two. Once they start school the milestones seem to slow and we tend to hand teachers a lot of the responsibility to provide our children feedback for their efforts. Make a promise to yourself to find just one opportunity every day to compliment each of your children for their efforts. Compliment them for trying a new food, starting or finishing homework more independently, helping around the house, remembering a chore, showing kindness and so on.

- How to compliment your child

  When complimenting your child try to focus the compliment on their effort (what they have done or said). So rather than saying, 'You won! You're the best gymnast' you might say, 'You won! That practice you've put in just paid off. I'm so proud of you!' Ideally it is best to avoid a focus on the product as this can contribute to perfectionism in children predisposed to this style of thinking.

Photocopiable resources now follow, and don't forget the online resources at www.whatsthebuzz.net.au!

After the Buzz . . . Lesson 16

CERTIFICATE OF GRADUATION

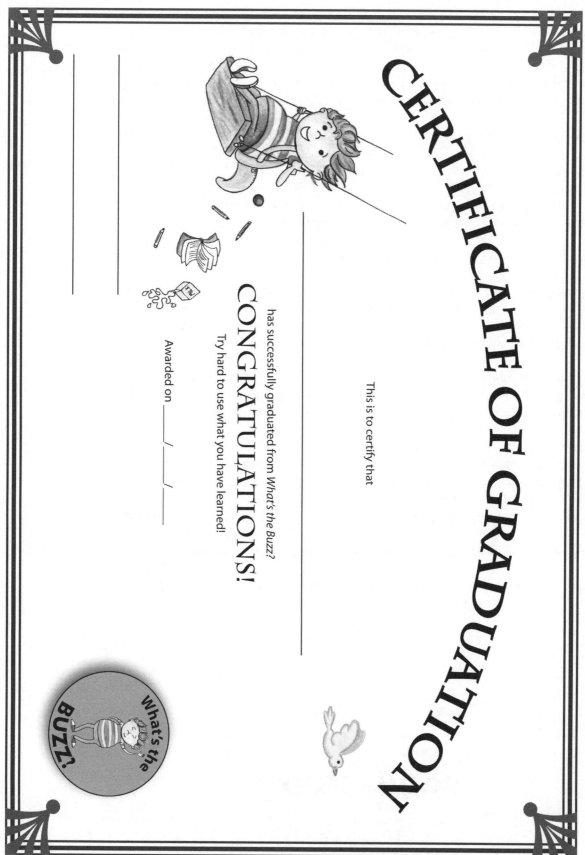

This is to certify that

_____

has successfully graduated from *What's the Buzz?*

CONGRATULATIONS!

Try hard to use what you have learned!

Awarded on _____

References

Attwood, T., 2007, *The Complete Guide to Asperger's Syndrome*, Jessica Kingsley Publishers, London.

Church, K., Gottschalk, C.M. and Leddy, J., 2003, 'Enhance social and friendship skills', *Journal of Intervention in School and Clinic*, 38 (5): 307–10.

Cornelius-White, J., 2007, 'Learner-Centered Teacher-Student Relationships Are Effective: A Meta-Analysis', *Review of Educational Research*, vol. 77, no. 1. pp. 113–43.

Cross, D., Shaw, T., Hearn, L., Epstein, M., Monks, H., Lester, L. and Thomas, L., 2009, 'Australian Covert Bullying Prevalence Study', Edith Cowan University, retrieved from www.deewr.gov.au/Schooling/NationalSafeSchools/Pages/research.aspx (accessed March 2010).

Diekstra, R.F., 2008, 'Effectiveness of school based social and emotional education programmes worldwide', in *Social and Emotional Education: An international analysis* (pages 255–312) Santander, Spain, retrieved from www.lions-quest.org/pdfs/EvaluationBotinEnglish.pdf (accessed November 2010).

Durlak, J.A., Weissberg, R.P., Dymnicki, A.B., Taylor, R.D. and Shellinger, K.B., 2008, 'Enhancing students' social and emotional learning promotes success in school: A meta-analysis', retrieved from www.casel.org (accessed November 2010).

Garcia Winner, M., 2003, *Thinking About You, Thinking About Me*, Jessica Kingsley Publishers, London.

Giorcelli, L., 2000, 'Wrap around', *ACTIVE Newsletter*, June 2000, Hyperactive Children's Association of Victoria, Yarraville, Victoria.

Godfrey, J., Pring, T., Gascoigne, M., 2005, 'Developing children's conversational skills in mainstream schools: An evaluation of group therapy', *Child Language Teaching and Therapy*, 21 (3): 251–62.

Hattie, J., 2009, *Visible Learning: A synthesis of over 800 meta-analyses relating to achievement*, Routledge, New York.

Hay, D., Payne, A. and Chadwick A., 2004, 'Peer relations in childhood', *Journal of Child Psychology and Psychiatry*, 45: 84–108.

Jenkins, H.J. and Batgidou, E., 2003, 'Developing social strategies to overcome peer rejection of children with Attention Deficit Hyperactivity Disorder', *Australian Journal of Learning Disabilities*, 8 (1): 16–24.

Payten, J., Weisberg, R., Derlak, J., Dyminicki, A., Taylor, R.D., Shellinger, K.M. and Pachan M., 2008, 'The positive impact for social and emotional learning for kindergarten to eighth grade students: Findings from three scientific reviews', *Executive Summary by Collaborative for Academic, Social and Emotional Learning*, retrieved from www.casel.org (accessed November 2010)

Rigby, K., 2002a, 'A meta-evaluation of methods and approaches to reducing bullying in pre-schools and in early primary school in Australia', Commonwealth Attorney-General's Department, Canberra.

Rigby, K., 2002b, *New Perspectives on Bullying*, Jessica Kingsley, London.

Rigby, K., 2004, 'What is bullying? Defining bullying: a new look at an old concept', retrieved from www.kenrigby.net/define.html (accessed March 2010).

Rigby, K. and Slee, P.T., 1999, 'Suicidal ideation among adolescent school children, involvement in bully/victim problems and perceived low social support', *Suicide and Life-threatening Behavior*, 29: 119–30.

Roffey, S., 2006, *Circle Time for Emotional Literacy*, Paul Chapman Publishing, London.

Scheier, M.F., 1986, 'Coping with stress: divergent strategies of optimists and pessimists', *Journal of Personality and Social Psychology*, 51 (6): 1257–64.

Scott, D., 2002, *Stress that Motivates: Self-talk secrets for success*, Nelson Education, Scarborough.

Seligman, M., 2002, *Authentic Happiness*, Free Press, New York.

Seligman, M., 2006, *Learned Optimism*, Pocket Books, New York.

Slee, P., Spears, B., Owens, L. and Johnson, B., 2008, 'Behind the scenes: insight into the human dimension of covert bullying', Hawke Research Institute for Sustainable Societies – University of South Australia and Centre for the Analysis of Educational Futures – Flinders University, SA, retrieved from www.deewr.gov.au/Schooling/NationalSafeSchools/Pages/research.aspx (accessed November 2010).

Stanley, F., 2008, *Risking Our Kids*, Perth: A Rymer Childs and Thunderbox Presentation, presented by Film Finance Corporation Australia.

Tse, J., Strulovitch, J., Tagalakis, V., Meng, L. and Fombonne, E., 2007, 'Social skills training for adolescents with Asperger syndrome and high functioning Autism', *Journal of Autism and Developmental Disorders*, 37: 1960–8.

Verduyn, C.M., Lord, W. and Forrest, G.C., 1990, 'Social skills training in schools: an evaluation study', *Adolescence*, 13: 3–16.